EQUITY
in the Classroom

ESSAYS FROM 10 EDUCATIONAL LEADERS:

MARIA ARMSTRONG

EDWIN D. BELL

FAY E. BROWN

CELESTE M. BRYANT

ROBERT L. GREEN

RACHEL HSIEH

TAI JONES

PAULA KNIGHT

KANDICE McLURKIN

ALONZO WESTBROOK

INTRODUCTION BY
JULIA E. TORRES

WHAT IT LOOKS LIKE AND HOW TO ACHIEVE IT

Acknowledgments

My deepest gratitude to Michael Haggen and Donald Creedon
for helping bring together this wonderful group of contributors,
who care so deeply about equity, especially in education.

Many thanks to Tara Welty, Kiini Salaam, Sue Macy, and Ourania
Papacharalambous for their editorial expertise.

Special thanks to Tonya Leslie, who did the sensitivity read
for all the essays—your insight and recommendations were invaluable.

—MLC

Photos ©: 9: kate_sept2004/Getty Images; 15: monkeybusinessimages/Getty Images; 36: Noun Project; 46: SDI Productions/Getty Images; 53: SeventyFour/Getty Images; 61: monkeybusinessimages/Getty Images; 65: Ridofranz/Getty Images; 70: STEEX/Getty Images; 110: Fly View Productions/Getty Images. All other photos © Shutterstock.com.

Editor: Maria L. Chang

Cover design: Tannaz Fassihi

Cover art: Shutterstock.com

Interior design: Maria Lilja

ISBN: 978-1-338-80787-5

Scholastic Inc., 557 Broadway, New York, NY 10012

CONTENTS

Introduction

by Julia E. Torres

To move toward a more equitable and just school system, we must first accept the fact that inequity (or injustice) is part of the human condition. For as long as there have been people on this planet, there have been environments and systems with the express purpose of creating inequity. Now, I know what you might be thinking: "Why would anyone intentionally want to create imbalance or inequity?" The answer is both simple and complex. In this compilation, you will read essays that attempt to provide answers about the ways in which inequitable systems and practices exist—and why—as well as essays that provide solutions about what we can do to dismantle them. In the end, however, it boils down to accepting just two truths: "Injustice is everywhere" and, in the words of civil rights activist Fannie Lou Hamer, "Nobody's free until everybody's free."

> What is true "equity" if we use the word so often that it comes to embody an idea no one can define, rather than concrete and commonplace practices?

So, what is freedom for today's students? Knowing that equity is a facet of inclusion, which in turn is a facet of the diamond of diversity, is important knowledge for educators to have. However, we are living in times when it is commonplace to hear and use "buzzwords" that simultaneously mean everything and nothing. What is true "equity" if we use the word so often that it comes to embody an idea no one can define, rather than concrete and commonplace practices?

Perhaps one of the first steps to truly understanding equity is to look closely at its opposite, inequity, and attempt to understand the conditions that brought about inequity in the first place. We know that educational systems can be both tools and products of colonization. Education is a means through which knowledge is passed from generation to generation, but also from one geographic region to another. Those who colonized lands often came from Europe and brought their religious, economic, and educational systems with them—and used them as justification for exercising power, occupying sacred land and spaces that were not theirs to occupy, and buying and trading human lives on the basis of racist principles. Knowing that this is our inheritance, we have to examine the ways in which we are all negatively impacted and spiritually imprisoned by inequity in order to overturn it. As we dismantle unconscious bias and step boldly toward acknowledging the past, we make way for a better, brighter future, one in which every child's humanity is honored, regardless of ethnic, cultural, linguistic, or racial background. It is also a future in which young people and those who serve them can participate in the pedagogy of healing, rather than one of emotional or spiritual denigration.

The essays in this book will challenge your thinking about what it means to live in a linguistically, ethnically, and culturally diverse society. The contributors are all people of color—eight of whom are Black, one Latina, and one Asian—and they come from different spheres of education. They are professors of education, district superintendents, school administrators, and classroom teachers, as well as a child psychologist, a social worker, and a strategic sales director for Scholastic. Each expert speaks from his or her own experience, so you'll hear different voices and different approaches to promoting equity. Some essays address equity from a theoretical, research-based standpoint, while others present practical strategies and action steps to be implemented in the classroom. Some offer solutions at the district and school level, while others encourage family and community engagement.

- Edwin D. Bell's essay, "The Pursuit of Equity in Education" (page 8), provides both historical context for why inequity exists as well as specific steps organizations can take to dismantle inequitable systems and create environments where all students can learn.

- Before we can undertake this work, however, it's crucial to begin transformation at the earliest stages, as Paula Knight explains in her essay, "The Powerful Promise of an Equitable Early Childhood Education" (page 21). She describes the systemic changes that must happen to lay the foundation for everything that follows.

- Kandice McLurkin's essay, "Building Equity Through Collective Teacher Efficacy" (page 32), provides a detailed example of the path we can follow to repair the ills of colonization and move toward a more unified future that develops the "mindset and skillset of both students and teachers . . .

reducing the guesswork and negative effect of unconscious bias that may deny students the opportunity to reach their full potential."

- To underscore this point, "Seeing and Teaching the Whole Child" (page 45), Fay E. Brown's essay, introduces the six key developmental pathways and emphasizes how teachers' attitudes and behavior can impact children's learning positively or negatively.

- Robert L. Green's essay, "Promoting High Student Achievement" (page 58), references the importance of holding high expectations for student achievement while involving the entire community—including families and caregivers—in educating the whole child.

- Alonzo Westbrook offers solutions to binary thinking in his essay, "Recognizing and Erasing Classroom Inequity" (page 64), by reminding us that equity in education includes equal access to a pedagogy of empowerment, equal access to and guarantee of high-quality instruction, and equal experiences with school systems and educators who are experts of their content areas and have been trained to serve young people.

- Rachel Hsieh's essay, "Instructional Equity: What, Why, and How" (page 75), lays out a clear pathway toward instructional equity in all content areas that offers students the chance to truly exercise full participatory citizenship.

- In "Spotlight on Third-Grade Literacy Proficiency for Black and Brown Youth" (page 88), Maria Armstrong focuses on developing the literacies of Black and Brown students as a method for achieving societal transformation that incorporates their strengths, rather than punishing them for not conforming to the system as it has always operated.

- As we strive toward creating educational communities that are "incubators for change," Celeste M. Bryant offers helpful self-reflection questions in her essay, "Equity and Justice in the Classroom and Beyond" (page 96). She recommends several ways to support young people working toward the development of critical consciousness, which—in this age of censorship, mass information, and mass disinformation—is needed now more than ever.

- Tai Jones invites us to move beyond the walls of our classrooms and school buildings in her essay, "Maximizing Field Trips to Close Opportunity Gaps" (page 113). She provides an innovative approach to building collective experiences in a world that is increasingly focused on separation and a system that has consistently rewarded individual success.

As we seek to do better by young people, we must recognize that many of them are already doing the work of building a better future. They are creating content via social media platforms and teaching one another about inequity and what it means to build a more just and more equal society through leading by example. As author, organizer, and educator Mariame Kaba has said, "Nothing that we do that is worthwhile is done alone." And so, know that you are not alone as you embark on the brave and curious work of understanding what true educational equity is and what you can do to bring it about, not just for those in your community but for untold generations of people who will come after we are long gone.

As diamonds are forged under great pressure, we must believe that to form an authentically (not performatively) just society we must all—individually and collectively—go through powerful transformations so that the diamond of diversity can shine its brightest. Much of the fear and division that has been a cornerstone of a deeply inequitable educational system is rooted in the erroneous belief that if one or some of us succeed at the cost of many others, this is an acceptable and inevitable price to pay.

Education should never be about creating barriers and building walls that divide us from one another or about controlling a narrative that perpetuates social hierarchy or one group's superiority. Instead, educators must always aim to be unified through our uniquely human capacity for sharing ideas and building upon the knowledge of our ancestors, drawing inspiration from the heavens and making it fit the circumstances and times in which we live.

Rather than remaining in a state of ideological separation, we can and we must do better. In the words of Gholdy Muhammad, author of *Cultivating Genius: An Equity Framework for Culturally and Historically Responsive Literacy*, "We're trying to help our students leave our schools and make the world a better place. We cannot keep repeating the same history." This is possible, of course, but we have to redefine who the "we" is in various contexts and why there has been such a historic precedent for creating division in the first place. When we reconcile our past with the present and seek out examples to follow—like those you will read within this collection—we reflect on our own positionality and responsibility for dismantling current conditions to lay a new foundation. In doing so, we take the first step on a path toward freedom—and that is a bold move, indeed.

Julia E. Torres is a language arts teacher in Denver, Colorado. As an advocate for all students and public education, Torres regularly participates in speaking engagements and facilitates workshops and professional conversations about equity, anti-bias/anti-racist education, culturally sustaining pedagogies, and literacy in the digital age. She also serves on several local and national boards and committees that promote educational equity and progressivism.

The Pursuit of Equity in Education

by Edwin D. Bell, Ed.D.

Horace Mann, who many consider the founder of public education, had a particular vision for public schools. His vision "included a common moral and political foundation, as well as the provision of opportunities for children from disadvantaged backgrounds to achieve self-sufficiency and use education to lift themselves from poverty" (Lynch, 2017). The pursuit of equity in education is simply the continued pursuit of Mann's vision for schools.

The purpose of this essay is to define equity in education; to explain why it is a necessary condition for the continuation of democracy in our society; to describe the context in which it must function; and to highlight some concepts and strategies that teachers can use to help achieve equity in their classrooms.

Background

For this essay, I will use the operational definition of *equity* that was developed by the Winston-Salem/Forsyth County School (WS/FCS) system as they addressed the achievement gap that is correlated to ethnicity, gender, and income in their school system.

Educational equity goes beyond basic principles of equality. A commitment to educational equity involves the removal of institutional barriers so that all students, regardless of their race, socioeconomic class, language proficiency, gender, sexual orientation, disability, or ethnic background, can benefit from all aspects of the learning environment. A commitment to equity in education involves raising achievement for all students, while also narrowing the gaps, with the goal to eliminate the gaps, and eliminating the racial and cultural disproportionalities that exist between the lowest and highest performing student groups in varying achievement areas within the Winston-Salem/Forsyth County school system. (WS/FCS, 2021, Policy Code 1100)

All students, regardless of race, gender, socioeconomic status, or language proficiency, benefit from a learning environment committed to equity.

The equity policy of WS/FCS is built on five pillars or administrative concerns:

1. **School Policy and Organization/Administration:** Analyze data through an equity lens to promote fairness and inclusion, and implement a set of established expectations, guidelines, and best practices.

2. **School Learning Environments:** Provide safe and well-maintained facilities and promote a variety of settings and contexts in which students will engage in academic and non-academic learning experiences that are representative of the school's community by race, ethnicity, language proficiency, gender, socioeconomic status, and disability.

3. **Academic Placement, Tracking, and Assessment:** Utilize achievement data to proportionately reflect the diverse demographics in special education, career and technical education, gifted education, and advanced placement programs.

4. **Professional Learning:** Increase the effectiveness of teachers, school leaders, and all K–12 staff in creating culturally responsive and equitable learning environments.

5. **Standards and Curriculum Development:** Implement culturally responsive and evidence-based instructional practices and integrate multicultural resources with diverse perspectives.

(WS/FCS, 2021, Policy Code 1100)

Classroom teachers play an essential and necessary part in the effective implementation of each pillar. What happens in the classroom determines the amount of equity in the school system.

Historical Context

In 2021, a White female elementary school teacher in Arkansas forced a Black, 5-year-old boy to clean out a toilet with his bare hands because he stopped up the toilet by using too much toilet paper. She initially told her principal that she did it to teach him not to stop up the toilet (Italiano, 2021). She later claimed that she did not know why she did it. Why did she think it was appropriate for her to treat a Black child—*any* child!—that way? Could she have been expressing an unconscious anti-Blackness that many White educators operate from, based on a long history of beliefs, laws, and values in our country that imply Black people are less than White people?

Long before the United States of America was formed, Virginia enacted the hereditary slave act in 1662:

> WHEREAS some doubts have arisen whether children got by any Englishman upon a negro woman should be slave or free, be it therefore enacted and declared by this present grand assembly, that all children born in this country shall be held bond or free, only according to the condition of the mother, . . . (NPS, n.d.)

Robert Beverley, a historian from early colonial times, reporting on laws regarding servants and enslaved people in Virginia, wrote:

> And if any slave resist his master or owner or other person, by his or her order, correcting such slave, and shall happen to be killed in such correction, it shall not be accounted felony; but the master, owner, and every such other person so giving correction shall be free and acquit of all punishment and accusation for the same, as if such accident had never happened; And also, if any negro, mulatto, or Indian, bond or free, shall at any time lift his

or her hand in opposition against any Christian, not being negro, mulatto, or Indian, he or she so offending shall, for every such offence proved by the oath of the party, receive on his or her bare back thirty lashes, well laid on; cognizable by a justice of the peace for that county wherein such offense shall be committed. (National Humanities Center, 2006)

Think about the norms and values that these state laws codified. What message did they send about human beings who were not White?

In the Dred Scott decision of 1857, the U.S. federal government made an even clearer statement about the value they put on African Americans. Chief Justice Roger Taney argued that African Americans were not people in terms of the Constitution of the United States.

> The framers, in his view, did not regard African Americans as being among the "people" for whose benefit and protection the new government was founded, notwithstanding the perfectly general language of the Declaration of Independence and of the preamble to the Constitution. (Urofsky, n.d.)

After the Civil War, Congress passed three constitutional amendments that were designed to change the conditions of formerly enslaved African Americans.

- **The 13th Amendment, ratified on December 6, 1865, abolished slavery in the United States of America.** The first section of the Amendment declares: "Neither slavery nor involuntary servitude, except as a punishment for crime whereof the party shall have been duly convicted, shall exist within the United States, or any place subject to their jurisdiction." The Amendment is unique in the Constitution because it bars every person from holding enslaved people or engaging in other forms of involuntary servitude, whereas most constitutional provisions only constrain or regulate the government. It is unique in another way as well: Although the Constitution obliquely acknowledged and accommodated slavery in its original text, the 13th Amendment was the first explicit mention of slavery in the Constitution (Green & McAward, 2021).

> After the Civil War, Congress passed three constitutional amendments that were designed to change the conditions of formerly enslaved African Americans.

- **Ratified on July 9, 1868, the 14th Amendment promised freedom to everyone born or naturalized in the United States.** "All persons born or naturalized in the United States, and subject to the jurisdiction thereof, are citizens of the United States and of the State wherein they reside.

No State shall make or enforce any law which shall abridge the privileges or immunities of citizens of the United States; nor shall any State deprive any person of life, liberty, or property, without due process of law; nor deny to any person within its jurisdiction the equal protection of the laws" (Interactive Constitution, 2021).

- **The purpose of the 15th Amendment, which was ratified on February 3, 1870, was to guarantee the right to vote to people who were formerly enslaved.** "The right of citizens of the United States to vote shall not be denied or abridged by the United States or by any State on account of race, color, or previous condition of servitude" (Interactive Constitution, 15th Amendment).

The presence of federal troops in the former Confederate states helped enforce these three amendments during the period of Reconstruction (1865–77). This was about to change, however, as a result of the highly disputed presidential election of 1876. Allies of Republican candidate Rutherford B. Hayes negotiated with the allies of Democratic candidate Samuel J. Tilden. If the Democrats conceded the election to Hayes, the Republicans would withdraw federal troops from the former Confederate states and end Reconstruction. The Democrats gave Hayes the victory.

This Compromise of 1877 ushered in the era of Jim Crow. Southern states used state law and terrorism to undermine the intent of the 13th, 14th, and 15th Amendments, denying African Americans the right to vote and forcing segregation of schools, restaurants, transportation, and more. With the implicit endorsement of the federal government, white supremacy prevailed in the former Confederacy. There was no successful attempt to oppose Jim Crow on a national level until the *Brown v. Board of Education of Topeka* decision in 1954.

The Supreme Court ruled in 1954 that separate but equal was in fact unconstitutional and that public schools should desegregate with all deliberate speed.

Brown v. Board of Education was a direct challenge to the doctrine of "separate but equal," which was established by the 1896 *Plessy v. Ferguson* decision that legalized segregation. Overturning this decision, the Supreme Court ruled in 1954 that separate but equal was in fact unconstitutional and that public schools should desegregate with all deliberate speed. Despite the legal significance of the ruling, it has never achieved the objective of integrating the nations' public schools. Several efforts have tried to undermine *Brown*. In the 1950s, Virginia politicians passed a group of laws that became known as Massive Resistance. They planned to close public schools that attempted to integrate, but this plan was defeated in the Virginia House of Delegates.

One of the extensive efforts to resist the *Brown* decision blossomed into a conservative strategy to alter the interpretation of the Constitution through the courts. In his article "Why School Integration Matters," Pedro Noguera (2019) argues that the promise of *Brown* has not been achieved due in part to subsequent court decisions and residential segregation, in which different groups are physically separated into different neighborhoods. For example, in the *Milliken v. Brady* case of 1974, the Supreme Court ruled that *de facto segregation*—segregation that occurs by circumstance, not by law—was constitutional (Hale, 2019). In other words, if a government entity did not segregate schools by law (known as *de jure segregation*) but schools became segregated anyway through other circumstances (e.g., residential segregation), then that segregation is legal. Noguera asserts that part of the reason *Brown* has not lived up to its promise "is also attributable to continued racism in our society, a lack of civic will, and the absence of political courage."

Concepts and Strategies for Implementing Equity

Several forces have obviously restrained Horace Mann's original vision for public education and continue to hinder the pursuit of equity in the classroom. Fortunately, we can implement specific strategies within our schools and classrooms to promote equity in education.

Provide High-Quality Education for ALL Children

Ronald Edmonds (1979) conducted and published a review of studies of poor, urban schools that did not have an achievement gap that was correlated with ethnicity or income. He concludes with these points:

> It seems to me what is left of this discussion are three declarative statements:
>
> a) We can, whenever we choose, successfully teach all children whose schooling is of interest to us;
>
> b) We already know more than we need to know to do that; and
>
> c) Whether or not we do it must finally depend on how we feel about the fact that we have not done it so far. (Edmonds, 1979)

Dobbie and Fryer (2011) conducted a large-scale study of the charter schools in the Harlem Children's Zone in New York. They reported that attendance at these charter schools could, by itself, reduce the achievement gap. A major source of the decrease in the achievement gap is the quality of the teaching. The teachers know their subjects well, they utilize a range of strategies to teach their subject, they are committed to their students, and they work together in a professional network. Their results seemed to support the conclusions that Edmonds had reached earlier:

> Harlem Children's Zone (HCZ), an ambitious social experiment, combines community programs with charter schools. We provide the first empirical test of the causal impact of HCZ charters on educational outcomes. Both lottery and instrumental variable identification strategies suggest that the effects of attending an HCZ middle school are enough to close the Black-White achievement gap in mathematics.

> The effects in elementary school are large enough to close the racial achievement gap in both mathematics and ELA. We conclude with evidence that suggests high-quality schools are enough to significantly increase academic achievement among the poor. Community programs appear neither necessary nor sufficient. (Dobbie & Fryer, 2011)

There were several things that made the schools in HCZ high quality. The students spent 200 percent more time on instruction. The teachers spent almost all their time on instruction and spent little time on trivial administrative tasks. In addition, the schools provided excellent two-way communication with families and caregivers. They also provided the counseling and social-emotional support that students needed. HCZ is not without its critics, however. One major criticism is that much of its funding, which made these achievements possible, came from private donations. It would be difficult to replicate the model across the country. "The challenge is to find lower-cost ways to achieve similar results in regular public schools," wrote Dobbie and Fryer (Otterman, 2010).

Become an Accomplished Teacher

Wang et al. (1993) conducted an analysis of 50 years of research on what factors impacted student learning. Their statistical analysis indicated that student ability was the most important factor. The second most powerful variable was the interaction among teachers and students in the classroom.

Kurt Lewin, who some consider the father of social psychology, proposed a simple, but complex formula to explain human behavior:

B = f (P, E)
i.e., behavior (B) is a function of the person (P) and their environment (E)

The complexity is in the operational definitions of P and E (Lewin, 2015). Individuals are not passive entities who are controlled by external forces. Who they are and who they want to be also impact how they behave. In addition, Weick (1976) argued that educational organizations are loosely coupled organizations, i.e., what happens in individual classrooms is difficult to control. Teachers have a great deal of autonomy in their classrooms. For example, each teacher develops the individual lesson plans that they decide to use to meet the objectives of the state-mandated curriculum.

A student is more likely to succeed when taught by an accomplished teacher.

In addition, Ladson-Billings (2009) described several case studies of individual accomplished teachers from diverse backgrounds who successfully taught African American students. Accomplished teachers can have a tremendous impact on their classrooms and their individual students.

What are the characteristics of an accomplished teacher? The National Board for Professional Teaching Standards (2021) recommends five core propositions for accomplished teachers.

> **Proposition 1:** Teachers are committed to their students and their learning.
>
> **Proposition 2:** Teachers know the subjects they teach and how to teach them.
>
> **Proposition 3:** Teachers are responsible for managing and monitoring student learning.
>
> **Proposition 4:** Teachers think systematically about their practice and learn from experience.
>
> **Proposition 5:** Teachers are members of learning communities.

These are professional characteristics that all teachers should emulate. I worked as a member of an action research team that helped develop these characteristics at Diggs-Latham Elementary School, a Title I school in the Winston-Salem/Forsyth County School System, over a three-year period. The teachers at Diggs-Latham met regularly as a grade-level learning committee to discuss ideas and suggestions to improve the performance of all the students across that grade level (Propositions 4 and 5). They assessed the individual learning needs for all the students in their grade level and met with the curriculum coordinator, assistant principal, and school principal on a quarterly basis to discuss the progress (Proposition 1). Several of the teachers were in graduate school or professional development programs (Proposition 2). They developed individualized growth plans for their students and brought tutors from a local fraternity to work with their 30 lowest-performing students (Proposition 3). The end-of-grade growth on scores in reading and mathematics (see Table 1, below) exceeded expectations by $< .001p$, which is highly significant (Powell et al., 2007).

Table 1. Diggs-Latham End-of-Grade Scores in Reading and Math from 1999–2002

	1999	2000	2001	2002
Grade 3	60.3	60.6	57.1	75.6
Grade 4	67.9	60.5	64.7	84.4
Grade 5	73.9	63.8	74.2	93.8

(Powell et al., 2007)

The five NBPTS (National Board for Professional Teaching Standards) core propositions for an accomplished teacher complement the five pillars of the educational equity policy outlined earlier in this essay (see Table 2).

Table 2. Relationship Among Pillars of Equity and NBPTS Core Propositions

PILLARS OF EQUITY	NBPTS CORE PROPOSITIONS
School Policy Organization/ Administration	**Proposition 4:** Teachers think systematically about their practice and learn from experience.
School Learning Environments	**Proposition 1:** Teachers are committed to their students and their learning.
Academic Placement, Tracking, and Assessment	**Proposition 3:** Teachers are responsible for managing and monitoring student learning.
Professional Learning	**Proposition 5:** Teachers are members of learning communities.
Standards and Curriculum Development	**Proposition 2:** Teachers know the subjects they teach and how to teach them.

Table 2 suggests that accomplished teachers can have a central role in the implementation of equity in the classroom.

Where to Start?

Build vocabulary and background knowledge. All public schools are open systems; that is, they constantly interact with their environment (Lunenburg, 2010). Given an open system's perspective, you can begin from various starting points and still get to the same desired end state.

However, I recommend vocabulary as a place to start in implementing equity in the classroom. Focusing on vocabulary allows all students to develop the mental schema and the operational vocabulary that are required to master the curriculum that is being taught. One of my graduate students, Ms. Kimberly Nelson, who taught in a Title I school that had a large population of multilingual learners, wanted to conduct her action research on aspects of the Sheltered Instruction Observation Protocol (SIOP), which was designed for multilingual learners.

> **Focusing on vocabulary allows all students to develop the mental schema and the operational vocabulary that are required to master the curriculum that is being taught.**

> The protocol is composed of 30 items grouped into three main sections: Preparation, Instruction, and Review/Assessment. The six items under Preparation examine the lesson planning process, including the language and content objectives, the use of supplementary materials, and the meaningfulness of the activities. Instruction is subdivided into six smaller categories: building background, comprehensible input, strategies, interaction, practice/application, and lesson delivery (Echeverria & Short, 2000).

Ms. Nelson decided to focus her action research on two of the instructional categories: building background and practice/application, based on her assessment of the needs of her students. As a third-grade teacher, she focused her efforts on revising her lesson plans for her reading and science activities. In her school, students are randomly assigned to one of five third-grade classes. Ms. Nelson wanted to determine if her intervention would have any impact on her students in comparison to the other four third-grade classes on their required end-of-grade tests in reading and mathematics. The chi-square test of independence yielded a p-value of 0.002 for reading and a p-value of 0.014 for mathematics on the difference in the scores among the class that received the intervention and the other four classes that did not. Simply put, the difference in student performance did not happen by chance (Nelson & Bell, 2012). The results of the two end-of-grade tests suggested that building background and a variety of practice/application strategies had a positive impact on student performance.

Increase instructional time and time on task. Dobbie and Fryer (2011) reported that children in the Harlem Children's Zone charter schools spent twice as much time on instructional tasks as other children in NYC public schools. This ties directly into the NBPTS Proposition 3 (Teachers are responsible for managing and monitoring student learning). Diggs-Latham Elementary School developed a collaborative relationship with the men of the Psi Phi Chapter of Omega Psi Phi Fraternity, Inc. They worked with the teachers, families, and students on individualized instructional plans and served as mentors for students. The 30 level-1 students—the lowest level in the state assessment system—who had extended instructional time through their tutors tested at or above grade level (Powell et al., 2007). The mentors/tutors also seemed to have a positive impact on student attitudes and behavior. I still remember one teacher telling me how much those little boys wanted "those men" to be proud of them.

Develop students' critical thinking skills. Although much of our educational bureaucracy is governed by performance on standardized tests, an individual's ability to function as a productive member of society is governed primarily by the ability to think critically, determine fact from fiction, and work collaboratively. One of the curriculum design strategies created to meet this need in the 1950s was Bloom's Taxonomy. It has been revised several times, but it provides a hierarchy of outcomes that illustrate at the upper levels how students should be able to use information. (See Figure 1 below.)

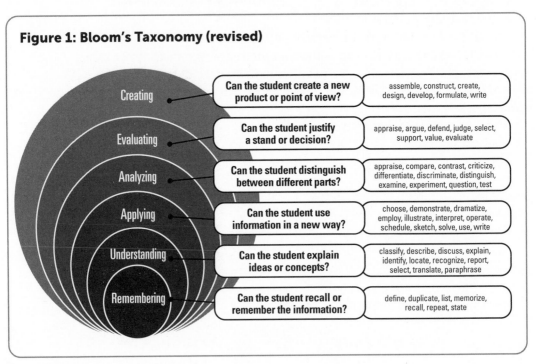

Figure 1: Bloom's Taxonomy (revised)

Level	Question	Verbs
Creating	Can the student create a new product or point of view?	assemble, construct, create, design, develop, formulate, write
Evaluating	Can the student justify a stand or decision?	appraise, argue, defend, judge, select, support, value, evaluate
Analyzing	Can the student distinguish between different parts?	appraise, compare, contrast, criticize, differentiate, discriminate, distinguish, examine, experiment, question, test
Applying	Can the student use information in a new way?	choose, demonstrate, dramatize, employ, illustrate, interpret, operate, schedule, sketch, solve, use, write
Understanding	Can the student explain ideas or concepts?	classify, describe, discuss, explain, identify, locate, recognize, report, select, translate, paraphrase
Remembering	Can the student recall or remember the information?	define, duplicate, list, memorize, recall, repeat, state

(CUTLA, 2015)

The model has continued to evolve to include other dimensions of knowledge, such as factual, conceptual, procedural, and metacognitive (CELT, 2017). This has led some researchers to define the upper levels of Bloom's Taxonomy as "critical thinking"—students not only use information to solve problems and create things, but are able to reflect on the thinking process as well (Alsaleh, 2020). Others expanded and modified Bloom's Taxonomy into higher-order thinking skills, or HOTS (Collins, 2014). There are multiple conceptual frameworks that have been and can be used in instructional design, but the goal is still the same: Produce students who can do well on standardized tests, but also find, assess, and use information to solve complex problems in all the roles that they will fulfill in our society.

Promote collaborative/ cooperative learning. Whichever paradigm you select, one of the instructional strategies that will help you achieve the proximal goal of your school system as well as the peripheral goal of our society is collaborative/cooperative learning.

Collaborative learning boosts students' critical thinking skills while promoting social skills.

Some researchers differentiate between the two by stating that cooperative learning is more faculty defined and driven, while collaborative learning has more student input in what is learned (Ravenscroft et al., 1999). Ravenscroft et al. argued that "the more actively students process information through student interaction, the more likely they are to learn and retain the information." The National Educational Association described the benefits of collaborative learning:

> Collaborative learning has been shown to not only develop higher-level thinking skills in students, but also boost their confidence and self-esteem as well. Group projects can maximize educational experience by demonstrating the material, while improving social and interpersonal skills. Students learn how to work with various types of learners and develop their leadership skills. (Gates, 2021)

Slavin and Oickle (1981) reported on the positive impacts of cooperative learning on all students, pointing out that cooperative learning also seemed to have additional benefits for Black students. One benefit for Black students in integrated groups is that their ability to succeed helped protect them from the predominant deficit model in many schools that Black and Brown students are "less than." I prefer cooperative learning because the instructor can shape the instructional outcomes more effectively by making sure that all the elements of Bloom's Taxonomy, critical thinking skills, and higher order thinking skills are addressed. In addition, it requires participants to listen carefully to their collaborators and to explain their own thinking clearly.

There are variety of collaborative learning strategies, but I have used a particular model called WebQuest (Dodge, 2017) with a wide range of age groups. Located at webquest.org, it allows you to implement all the objectives of Bloom's Taxonomy, critical thinking skills, and higher order thinking skills. The website includes guidelines that help you to develop your own WebQuests to meet the needs of your students and their situation.

Conclusion

Regardless of where you decide to start in your classroom/subsystem and what you start with, you are facing well-organized and well-financed efforts to put chains on democracy and a return to the era of *Plessy v. Ferguson* (MacLean, 2018). Student by student, classroom teachers can help break those chains. Accomplished teachers are a necessary condition not only for equity in the classroom but also for achieving Horace Mann's original vision for public education. Become an accomplished teacher!

Edwin Dewey Bell, Ed.D., was born in Boston, Massachusetts. He attended the Boston Public Schools. Currently, he is a professor emeritus of education at Winston-Salem State University, North Carolina, and a board member for Action4Equity. He has more than 40 years of experience as an administrator and a faculty member in psychology and educational leadership in higher education.

The Powerful Promise of an Equitable Early Childhood Education

by Paula Knight, Ed.D.

Straight out of college and preparing for my first day in the classroom, I was the picture of professionalism. My long hair was cinched into an updo. I pulled on a white silk blouse and topped it with a perfectly fitted dark-blue suit. I paired the ensemble with black heels and added a gold bracelet with a good-luck charm. I was ready for my first day as an early childhood teacher!

As I prepared for this very important role, I drew upon my own middle-school experiences and real-life role models: my teachers, Ms. Primm, Ms. Zimmerman, and Ms. Evans. Ms. Evans, in particular, had a distinct style about her and walked with her hand on her hip. That pose would have looked haughty or intimidating on others. However, when Ms. Evans glided around the room, she simply and softly commanded my attention. I wanted to learn everything she had to teach. I wanted to make her proud. I wanted to grow up and be like Ms. Evans.

Six hours and 18 preschoolers later, I was sore from sitting in tiny desks and doing floor work. My feet hurt from rapid-fire sprints to keep up with my little charges. When I look back at that first day I smile, thinking of how ill-prepared I was. I also realize how it shaped me for what was to come. Having studied far more about how to teach than about how young children actually learn, I was outmatched that first day. In my imagination, my students would sit like little sponges, absorbing all the knowledge I was more than prepared to share. I also thought that my excitement, enthusiasm, and love for my job would make all the difference for them. I was half right.

Undaunted, I went back the next day wearing jeans, a dark shirt, flat shoes—and my heart on my sleeve. For two years, I folded my body into those small desks, sat cross-legged on the floor, acted out books, taught lessons, and assured parents that their children were little geniuses. That is how I saw them—each shining face full of wonderment and potential. We read books, drew pictures, and formed letters and words on the chalkboard. In the end, those little children were my teachers. I learned that what every child needs is time, space, and materials to support his or her transformation into a little learner. I also learned that satisfying children's needs was much easier said than done.

Early Childhood Education vs. Day Care: What Is the Difference?

Many prospective parents start searching their communities for day-care centers well before their children are born. They want to make sure that their child has the best educational jump start they can provide to ensure kindergarten readiness. However, the single most important thing parents can provide for their children comes a little further down the road. It is early childhood education (ECE).

Science tells us that children's brains are still forming at ages 3 and 4. We know that the growing human body needs fresh air, nutritious food, and tender loving care. Add to that an environment that encourages young ones to be inquisitive, to get their hands dirty, and to build on what interests them—and you have early childhood education. Day-care centers provide a safe and fun place for children to learn and explore while socializing with one another during play. Early childhood education offers all these things and more.

Three- and 4-year-olds benefit from a constructive and balanced instructional environment in an accredited early childhood education facility, not day care. I am a public-school advocate, but I acknowledge that Montessori schools are especially good at building gross motor skills and developing critical thinking, which influence cognitive development. But that method is not for everyone. I myself created a preschool program in which children learn at their own pace and benefit from individual work plans. Every child's educational needs may be different, but early childhood education is for every child. It delivers a balanced schedule of structured activities designed to actively prepare children for kindergarten.

Kindergarten readiness is not easy to define. Typical development varies among children between the ages of 3 and 5 years of age, and a child's progress in a particular skill does not necessarily translate into development in other skills. We must remember a child's development is rooted in milestones that help make kindergarten readiness successful and sustainable throughout the primary years of schooling. Some milestones include:

- demonstrating curiosity in learning something new
- demonstrating the ability to explore through senses
- learning how to cooperate and take turns
- print awareness
- color recognition
- sound differentiation

(Mayo Clinic, 2021).

Understanding that these skills develop and strengthen over time, we can define readiness as a process, not an end goal. Providing an early educational experience in a structured environment prepares children to learn.

The fact is, well-educated parents and parents with resources are very likely to understand the importance of providing early learning opportunities for their children, whether in preschool or at home. If they decide to homeschool their 3- and 4-year-olds—teach them numbers

Early childhood education provides balanced instructional activities in fun and engaging ways.

and the alphabet, read to them regularly, take them to the zoo or museums, and so on—there is a good chance their children will enter kindergarten with an advantage, even without the help of a formal early learning program.

Likewise, parents with fewer resources—less time, money, or education—also want the best for their children. Unfortunately, they are not always able to stay home and provide the one-to-one support young children need to establish early learning habits. It is for these families that early childhood education becomes critically important.

How Do We Ensure Equity for All Children?

Early childhood programs across this country demonstrate stratification of our society by race and class, compounded by centuries of systemic racism among Black and Indigenous people (Children's Defense Fund, 1995). Particularly in urban communities, there is an increasing need for ECE. One can argue that in lower socioeconomic areas, there are minimal resources that can support educational preparation. People living in poverty are often in survival mode— they prioritize food, clothing, and shelter. Instructional resources are often not considered a priority at home, with many families asking, "Isn't that the school's responsibility?" All things being equal, perhaps it would be.

If we, as a nation, carry a moral obligation to protect and care for the children in our country, we need to provide equal access for childcare as well as dynamic early childhood programs for all.

To address such inequities, a strong and sustainable early childhood program must be on a continuum of ongoing support, beginning at birth. If we, as a nation, carry a moral obligation to protect and care for the children in our country, we need to provide equal access for childcare as well as dynamic early childhood programs for all. The frailties of the current educational system (even before the COVID pandemic hit) have positioned educational leaders to look deeply into this crisis of just how fairly and equitably we educate all children.

Age Matters

Before we start to look at surface practice, let's consider the notion of equitable practices in early childhood education by analyzing the compulsory age requirements across the country. (See Table 3, pages 25–26.)

Many parents choose not to send their children to school until it is mandated by the state. This becomes a disadvantage for children. In Missouri, for example, school is not mandated until first grade. During the pandemic, families' mistrust of science and fear of exposing their babies to illness were really all they needed to justify keeping their children at home for as long as they could. Not required by law, kindergarten was considered unnecessary, and the popularity for preschool began to wane. In 2020, the year the pandemic hit, we lost 29 percent of our early childhood (P3's and P4's) population.

Early childhood is a critical time, and the experiences children have in these formative years play a pivotal role in preparing them for future success. It is essential that educators and other key stakeholders, such as parents, schools, and governing bodies, recognize the integral role that early childhood education plays in lifelong learning. If we know that it's important to instill a love for continuous learning as soon as possible, why would we not formally encourage school for 3- and 4-year-olds? Mandating kindergarten readiness is a future-forward opportunity for all children.

Until our federal government inserts policy that lowers the required school attendance age for children, equitable practices will continue to suffer. When we examine the chart that outlines age requirements by state, coupled with inconsistent requirements for public versus private institutions, the "starting and finishing" lines will always remain biased.

Table 3: Compulsory school attendance laws, minimum and maximum age limits for required free education, by state: 2017

(National Center for Education Statistics, 2017)

State	Age of required school attendance	Minimum age limit to which free education must be offered
Alabama	6 to 17	5
Alaska	7 to 16	5
Arizona	6 to 16	6
Arkansas	5 to 18	5
California	6 to 18	5
Colorado	6 to 17	5
Connecticut	5 to 18	5
Delaware	5 to 16	5
District of Columbia	5 to 18	5
Florida	6 to 16	4
Georgia	6 to 16	5
Hawaii	5 to 18	5
Idaho	7 to 16	5
Illinois	6 to 17	4
Indiana	7 to 18	5
Iowa	6 to 16	5
Kansas	7 to 18	5
Kentucky	6 to 18	5
Louisiana	7 to 18	5
Maine	7 to 17	5
Maryland	5 to 18	5

State	Age of required school attendance	Minimum age limit to which free education must be offered
Massachusetts	6 to 16	3
Michigan	6 to 18	5
Minnesota	7 to 17	5
Mississippi	6 to 17	5
Missouri	7 to 17	5
Montana	7 to 16	5
Nebraska	6 to 18	5
Nevada	7 to 18	5
New Hampshire	6 to 18	—
New Jersey	6 to 16	5
New Mexico	5 to 18	5
New York	6 to 16	5
North Carolina	7 to 16	5
North Dakota	7 to 16	5
Ohio	6 to 18	5
Oklahoma	5 to 18	5
Oregon	6 to 18	5
Pennsylvania	8 to 17	6
Rhode Island	5 to 18	5
South Carolina	5 to 17	5
South Dakota	6 to 18	5
Tennessee	6 to 18	5
Texas	6 to 19	5
Utah	6 to 18	5
Vermont	6 to 16	5
Virginia	5 to 18	5
Washington	8 to 18	5
West Virginia	6 to 17	5
Wisconsin	6 to 18	4
Wyoming	7 to 16	5

Promoting Equity in Early Childhood Classrooms

Creating an equitable classroom is essential to a productive learning environment. Creating equity in a classroom is complex. As educators, how can we create an environment in which all children, regardless of skin color, background, and experiences can thrive? Here are a few ideas.

1. **Make time for reflection.** As educators, we tend to bring our own beliefs into the classroom without reflecting on how this may impact our students. Everyone has "blind spots," but to overcome this we must be conscious of these issues and learn how turn them into a positive learning experience for all children.

2. **Learn to diversify the written and taught curriculum.** Children must be exposed to a wide variety cultures. Seek books and teaching resources that reflect your students' various cultural backgrounds.

3. **Hold every child to high standards.** Regardless of each child's background, maintaining high expectations is important and sets the tone for all learners.

4. **Recognize and accommodate various learning needs and disabilities.** Different children have different learning needs. Creating an equitable learning environment begins with educators knowing each child's learning needs and making the necessary accommodations to ensure academic success.

Radical Change in Teacher Training

Now, let's consider the way we compensate, respect, and honor educators. Our international colleagues experience far different levels of respect than we do here in the United States. In China, Switzerland, and Finland, parents and communities revere their educational systems. They respect educators and hold them in the same high esteem typically afforded those in the medical or law fields in our country. *Please take a moment to reflect on how we characterize educators in the American school systems.*

The pandemic highlighted the importance of teachers, and there was deafening applause to every educator across this nation for their unwavering commitment and dedication to walking into the unknown for their students. Let us not forget, many of these teachers have children of their own, who needed them as much as their "school" children did.

Having realized the value and importance of our educators, advocates and practitioners are now looking at how we tackle the issue (that is here to stay) of credentialing and even on-the-job training. Not all credentialing programs are the same, but the key question remains: *How can we redesign our teacher training programs to focus on equitable practices, including instructional practices that support multilingual learners, students with disabilities, and behavioral health?*

Before colleges and universities begin to look at retooling their degree programs and internal structures, one important word comes to mind: *radical*. We need to create a radical design—"learning reimagined through radical thinking for equitable futures" (Imaginable Futures, 2020)—to the early childhood preparation program that is unlike what anyone has seen or experienced, if our educational system is truly to meet the needs of our youngest learners. Today's teaching and learning environment is satisfactory at best—our children deserve more and better. We must look at the teacher preparation programs and the continuous credentialing teacher programs. Professional learning must be current, forward thinking, and ongoing.

To offer such change in design and practice, colleges and universities are overhauling their degree programs with competency and project-based practices. However, they also need to analyze their teaching staff to be reflective of the changes we wish to see. As a system, we must establish a more conscious effort to attract, recruit, and retain culturally responsive faculty who share the philosophy for sustainable change.

So much work still needs to be done if we are seeking to sustain equitable early childhood classrooms and equitable teacher programs, specifically in mindset and teaching practices across this country. Additionally, educators must reflect on their own teaching methods and build a new framework for thinking—one that advocates for the rights of children and ensures children have voice, rights, choice, and power within curriculum decision-making. While teaching traditional skills, such as reading, writing, and numeracy, is still important, educators must also recognize the importance of developing dispositions for learning and life skills, which will help learners become productive caretakers of our future.

Equitable Funding

When I first arrived as a teacher in a large, urban Midwest school district, I was already aware of the disparity that existed when it came to delivering instruction in the county and city schools. Having grown up in an upper middle-class family, I noticed one glaring sign of inequity: The Parents as Teachers (PAT) program is more prevalent in middle to upper socioeconomic classes and not so much in urban centers. PAT is a support program in which a parent educator conducts home visits to screen for any developmental delays and document developmental milestones in children. Such support gives children and families the opportunity to address developmental delays in an effort to ensure success in early learning milestones.

At the time, our district served 20,000 students in 60 schools, including some of the top-performing schools in the state as well as some of the lowest-performing schools. There was a great disparity in socioeconomic status district-wide, and approximately 5 percent of our students did not have a stable home. We were behind by zip code (our students from the poorest areas) and by state funding formula, which was different from that of the neighboring and rural districts. Not only did our public schools receive less funding overall, further restrictions and demands weakened our ability to provide additional or enhanced services for those who needed it. With our growing population of special-needs students, equity once again floats out of reach. How would we ever be able to ensure that every child has what he or she needs to succeed in school and in life? Our parents demand—and deserve—more.

If we truly believe in the value of early childhood education, we must expand our investment in programs that serve the needs of all children and their families. Early childhood education must be fully funded and supported by our state education system. Why should school districts be required to secure outside funding to send their youngest children to school? Why would we not want to feed young children's curiosity and imagination with materials and activities that will stay with them for life? Now more than ever, it is critical that our funding formulas are equitable and earmarked specifically for early childhood education and kindergarten readiness.

Equity in the Time of COVID-19

Generally, people who decide to make a career in education care deeply for children and want what is best for every one of them. Deep down, we know that "what's best" for one is not necessarily what is best for another. For many school administrators, the concept of equity in education has been an intangible idea—an elusive thought bubble hanging over our heads. We know that every child deserves to receive what he or she needs to succeed, but we just cannot seem to pull together the many resources we need to deliver on this promise.

That is, until the pandemic forced schools across the globe to close and propelled us into creating an instructional world of virtual structures and practices. In 2020, the pandemic was the flash point that ignited a passion for equity assurance that lay heavy inside many of us. The pandemic and all its challenges to life, liberty, and learning further burdened families—many of whom were living below the poverty level and struggling day-to-day.

At the time, I was chief academic officer for a large, urban school district and was very aware of the fact that the world was actually seeing what before was only a concept. For years, we had considered the word *equity* and what it meant to our district. We made it a "pillar" of our strategic plan. We tried to define it; we tried to describe what it looked like; and we even created checks and balances for how it would be measured. The definitions were either too vague or too detailed to be practical. In addition, rather than describing what it would look like, we found ourselves focusing more on the other *face*—the absence of equity.

During the pandemic, equity was finally out in the center of the room as we brainstormed ways to deliver learning alternatives, equipment, and materials to thousands of students scattered across my district and the city's nine-mile footprint. We learned that in many areas (rural, urban, and suburban), students did not have immediate access to devices and the internet at the onset of the pandemic. This sounded the alarms on the inequities across the country. We needed to address these inequities immediately, rather than delay any plans to "level the field" for all. As much as possible, we provided one-to-one technology devices and distance-learning opportunities for students and teachers to begin making interpersonal connections during a time when personal connections were stalled.

Even as the pandemic dies down, our new practices of virtual instruction and one-to-one technology for all students should not fade along with it. My fear is that we will lose the momentum of implementing virtual access for all that we gained during the pandemic. My hope is that we harness the idea that equity in education will remain possible for all children.

Preserving Early Childhood Education

If you believe that every child deserves a great start in life, no matter where he or she lives and no matter the parents' education or socioeconomic level, then you believe in early childhood education. Done right, early childhood education is the great equalizer.

Early childhood is a period of milestone experiences for all people, regardless of zip code, color, or creed. By the time this period has concluded, children will have formed conceptions of themselves as social beings, as critical thinkers, and as language users, and they will have come to specific yet important decisions about their own abilities and their own worth (Donaldson et al., 1983). I am reminded of the book, *All I Really Needed to Know I Learned in Kindergarten,* by Robert Fulghum (2004). The author takes a lighthearted look at how and when we learn the skills we carry through life. This is when the love and appreciation for learning begins. This is true for skills, such as socialization and self-regulation, which are taught and learned in an early childhood classroom.

Preschool is where the fireworks happen. It's when children start to grasp more complex concepts, and you can see sparks fly when their eyes come alive with, "I got it!" There is such power in finding out that you have the ability to do it— whatever *it* is—all by yourself! That power sets the tone for becoming a lifelong learner. In fact, 3- and 4-year-olds will learn in preschool what works for them: *How do I get what I want or need? Do I try to please the teacher? Do I throw a tantrum when upset? Do I share my toys freely with others?*

Children carry these learned behaviors with them all through school and into their adult lives. We have the opportunity to make sure that young children learn the correct ways to interact with other children and adults, to solve problems, and to effectively and peacefully advocate for themselves and others. Preschool gives little people the foundation—the confidence—they need to succeed in school and to grow up to be productive members of our global society. And, if we've done our jobs correctly, perhaps they will grow up to be great adults.

> **Early childhood is a period of milestone experiences for all people, regardless of zip code, color, or creed.**

Paula Knight, Ed.D., is the superintendent of schools for the Jennings School District in Missouri. Prior to that, she was deputy superintendent/chief academic officer for the Saint Louis Public Schools. Dr. Knight began her education career in 1994 as a classroom teacher at Hamilton Elementary School, in Missouri. She has served as an instructional coach and principal at Waring Academy of Basic Instruction and Washington & Euclid Montessori School and as the executive director of curriculum and instruction K–12, associate superintendent of elementary schools/early childhood and chief of staff (interim). Dr. Knight has a bachelor of arts degree in elementary education from Saint Louis University and master of arts and doctorate in Education Leadership degrees from the University of Missouri–St. Louis.

Building Equity Through Collective Teacher Efficacy

by Kandice McLurkin, M.Ed.

Back when I was the principal of a diverse student population at Cienega Elementary School in Los Angeles, I received a copy of Geneva Gay's book, *Culturally Responsive Teaching: Theory, Research, and Practice*. I remember thinking how unfortunate it was that I might not have the time to read this book that could give me insight on how to support my struggling African American and multilingual learner populations. To remedy that, I found a few accountability buddies with whom to form a book-study group. As we delved into the book, I was pleasantly surprised to see that Gay included positive achievement data supporting culturally responsive teaching (CRT). She defines *culturally responsive pedagogy* as "the use of cultural knowledge, prior experiences, frames of reference, and performance styles of ethnically diverse students to make learning more relevant to and effective for them" (Gay, 2018). I wanted positive achievement outcomes for my underserved populations, but was still left with the questions: *How does this translate into effective* *day-to-day classroom practices that can accelerate learning for all students? How can we develop our capacity to serve our underserved standard English learner population?*

Our staff participated in Los Angeles Unified School District's Academic English Mastery Program (AEMP), a comprehensive, research-based program that supports teachers in addressing the language and literacy needs of African American, Mexican American, Hawaiian American, and Native American students for whom dominant/standard English is not native. The program offers professional development, instructional materials and strategies, and lesson plans to facilitate the language learning of culturally diverse students. In addition, the staff created and implemented a multi-tiered system of support (MTSS) for academics as well as for behavior. The result was double-digit gains on standardized tests for all subgroups, illustrating the effectiveness of applying CRT concepts into day-to-day classroom practices. In addition, our school became a model for the positive behavior interventions and supports (PBIS) framework and a cohesive staff.

I went on to become the administrative coordinator of AEMP, supporting more than 115 school sites. In 2019, AEMP was selected as one of 57 recipients of California's leading educational honors, the Golden Bell Award. These awards are presented by the California School Boards Association to promote excellence in public education and school board governance by recognizing outstanding programs and governance practices. The awards reflect the depth and breadth of education programs and governance decisions supporting these programs that are necessary to address students' changing needs.

Most educators would agree that effective pedagogical strategies all begin with a thorough understanding of the vast uniqueness of the students we serve. This can be a daunting task for teachers to undertake individually. Students' unique characteristics can include, but are not limited to, learning speed and styles, prior knowledge, and cultural as well as linguistic differences. With regard to prior knowledge, for example, does the student have the fundamental skills needed to develop new skills? In today's classrooms, there may be tremendous diversity in terms of culturally based learning needs and home- and academic-language proficiency. These are some of the challenges that educators need to consider when they strive to create a learning environment in which all students thrive.

To support this work, we need to utilize three frameworks to guide our actions and capitalize on the cultural and linguistic assets of all students. These three frameworks are:

1. Equity
2. Multi-Tiered System of Support (MTSS)
3. Culturally Responsive Teaching (CRT)

When teachers build with the strength of their colleagues to improve teaching and learning, they can change the trajectory and lives of all students. Creating a school-wide multi-tiered system of support builds collective teacher efficacy.

Collective teacher efficacy (CTE) refers to a shared belief that the school staff working together can have a positive effect on student achievement, despite other influences and limitations that challenge their success. According to John Hattie's *Visible Learning* synthesis of over 800 meta-analyses, the study of studies relating to student achievement, CTE matters more to positive student outcomes than any other aspect of schooling (2012). CTE is strongly correlated with student achievement and has the potential to triple the speed of learning. Therefore, a school-wide, classroom-implemented MTSS that is based on CTE may be the most powerful tool to achieve academic equity in the classroom for all students.

Academic Equity Defined

Equity can be defined as "fair outcomes, treatment, and opportunities" for all students.

What does that look like at a school? How can a school work toward becoming an equity-centered organization? Educators need to create a shared vision for the metrics they will use to determine if they are working toward equity and giving all students the support they need to ensure:

- positive outcomes on gatekeepers, such as standardized tests;
- a respectful learning environment in which to thrive; and
- opportunities that are rigged for success.

But first, educators must develop a shared understanding of what the words "fair outcomes, treatment, and opportunity" mean.

Let's begin with the word **fair**. Is it fair? When considering whether something is "fair," ask yourself: *Is it good enough for my child/family/friends?*

Next, let's define **fair outcomes**. What are "fair outcomes"? How do you measure the impact of your teaching and learning? Ask yourself again: *Are the results on standardized tests for all subgroups (as well as re-classification rates for multilingual learners, movement on progress monitoring, attendance, and so on) good enough for my child, family, and friends?*

Now, let's move on to the definition of **fair treatment**. When determining what "fair treatment" looks like, ask yourself: *What will we use to measure student, community, and teacher satisfaction?* (For example, positive behavioral interventions and supports [PBIS] data review of office referrals, suspensions, and expulsions; satisfaction surveys; and so on.) *Would those results be good enough for my children, family members, or other people I care about?*

Finally, let's define **fair opportunities**. Again, ask yourself: *Do we have opportunities that are rigged for success for all students?* These could include: seeing oneself in the school environment and curriculum; classroom libraries with males of color as protagonists; strengths and challenges attended to with school-wide activities and focus on enrichment and intervention; electives; AP courses taught by highly effective teachers; the three tiers of prevention for reading failure; and so on.

> When considering whether something is "fair," ask yourself: Is it good enough for my child/family/ friends?

All of these ideas are captured in the acronym FOTO: fair outcomes, treatment, and opportunities.

Looking Through Various Lenses of Equity

When developing a multi-tiered system of support that is culturally and linguistically responsive, it is essential that we help build the capacity of administrators, teachers, counselors, school psychologists, and the school community to examine existing policies, practices, and school structures from an equity framework perspective. Equity means giving each student exactly what he or she needs to succeed; therefore, lenses to start with could include but are not limited to:

- **Academic equity:** Developing values, beliefs, and mindsets that lead to "good first instruction" with an integrated, data-driven focus on improving outcomes for all students on a continuous basis.
- **Resource equity:** Examining current resource allocation and use of resources (e.g., curriculum, staff, budget, professional development) to enable all teachers and students to thrive.
- **Systemic equity:** Implementing inclusive and equitable structures, systems, and policies (e.g., positive behavior support, progressive discipline, language development schedules, yard supervision, and hiring practices).
- **Climate equity:** Taking actions to integrate and foster understanding of social-emotional, cultural, and academic needs to build a climate of mutual respect that results in developing lifelong resilient, confident, and independent learners throughout the school.

These equity lenses or frameworks can help educators disrupt or eliminate inequities and rebuild with evidence-based practices that can accelerate learning and promote academic excellence for all students at the school site. To facilitate the process of identifying equity assets and challenges, we can refer to John Hattie's *Visible Learning[plus] 250+ Influences on Student Achievement*. It identifies not only factors that accelerate academic achievement, but also elements that have a negative impact on academic achievement and that need to be disrupted. Because we can't reclaim time lost, schools must focus on what works best to optimize teaching and student learning. Many schools will be tempted to address unfinished learning, or skills normally mastered by this time, by looking to remedial programs. But research released by the Thomas B. Fordham Institute in spring 2021, *The Acceleration Imperative,* makes the argument in support of accelerated learning rather than remediation. It means going forward, not backward. Devoting the bulk of classroom time to classroom instruction at grade level or higher gives all students access to a rich, high-quality curriculum in English language arts, mathematics, as well as other core areas of instruction.

MTSS as a Vehicle to Achieve Student Equity

A multi-tiered system of support offers the potential to create needed systemic change through intentional design and redesign of services and support. This helps educators quickly identify and match the needs of all students for academic, behavioral, and social success. It fosters collective teacher and staff efficacy, providing an understanding of how all educators on the school site can work together to ensure equitable access and opportunities that are rigged for success for all students.

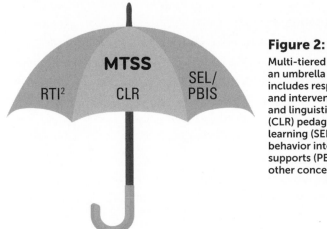

Figure 2: What Is MTSS?

Multi-tiered system of support is an umbrella or framework that includes response to instruction and intervention (RTI[2]), culturally and linguistically responsive (CLR) pedagogy, social-emotional learning (SEL), and positive behavior interventions and supports (PBIS), in addition to other concepts.

Every state and school district has guidelines on what should be included in a strong MTSS. Many contain the same core attributes, such as time for collaboration, high-quality instruction by effective teachers, and a data-analysis process. But let's look at California for guidance on equity because of its size and diversity. California's diverse population includes consideration of more than 90 languages and cultures, standard English learners, multilingual learners, students who are deaf and bilingual in ASL (American Sign Language), advanced learners, students living in poverty, migrant students, students with disabilities, and LGTBQ+ students who benefit from differentiated instruction. The California Department of Education defines MTSS as an integrated, comprehensive framework that focuses on Common Core state standards, core instruction, differentiated learning, student-centered learning, individualized student needs, and the alignment of systems necessary for all students' academic, behavioral, and social success.

10 Core Components of a Strong MTSS/RTI^2 Plan

(California Department of Education, 2021; cde.ca.gov)

1. **High-quality classroom instruction:** Students receive high-quality, standards- and research-based, culturally and linguistically relevant instruction in their classroom setting from highly qualified teachers.

2. **High expectations:** It is evident in the school and district cultures that everyone shares a belief that every student—including students of poverty, students with disabilities, multilingual learners, and students representing all ethnicities—can learn.

3. **Assessments and data collection:** An integrated data collection and assessment system that includes universal screening, diagnostics, and progress monitoring informs decisions that are appropriate for each tier of service delivery.

4. **Positive behavioral support:** School staff members use school-wide and classroom research-based positive behavioral supports for achieving important social and learning outcomes.

5. **Research-based interventions:** When monitoring data indicate a lack of progress, an appropriate research-based intervention is implemented. The interventions are designed to increase the intensity of the students' instructional experience.

6. **Problem-solving systems approach:** Collaborative teams use a problem-solving process and method to identify problems, develop interventions, and evaluate the effectiveness of the intervention in a multi-tiered system of service delivery.

7. **Fidelity of program implementation:** Student success in the response to instruction and intervention (RTI^2) framework requires fidelity of implementation. That means the content and instructional strategies specific to the learning and/or behavioral needs of each student are delivered and implemented as intended.

8. **Staff development and collaboration:** All school staff members are trained in assessments, data analysis, programs, and research-based instructional practices and positive behavioral support. Site grade-level or interdisciplinary teams use a collaborative approach to analyze student data and work together in developing, implementing, and monitoring the intervention process.

9. **Family involvement:** The involvement and active participation of families and caregivers at all stages of the instructional and intervention process are essential to improving the educational outcomes of their students. Families and caregivers are kept informed of the progress of their students in their native language or other mode of communication, and their input is valued in making appropriate decisions.

10. **Specific learning disability determination:** The RTI[2] approach may be one component to determine specific learning disability, as addressed in the Individuals with Disabilities Education Act of 2004 statute and regulations. As part of determining eligibility, the data from the RTI[2] process may be used to ensure that a student has received research-based instruction and interventions.

Multi-tiered system of support is a process designed to realign resources to meet the academic, behavioral, and social-emotional needs of all students by integrating evidence-based best practices and resources, then streamlining them into a school-wide plan (e.g., positive behavior interventions and supports, response to instruction, culturally and linguistically responsive pedagogy, pro social-emotional curriculums, restorative justice). MTSS maximizes learning by matching student needs to differentiated instruction through a systematic use of data, a collaborative problem-solving process, and the development of collective teacher efficacy. MTSS will look different at every school and is flexible to what each student requires.

Additionally, there are three tiers of support that help ensure academic, behavioral, and social success. Developing the three tiers of support is fundamental to MTSS/RTI[2] when used to match the level of instruction students need to their level of support. Table 4 (page 39) provides a model of what a three-tiered system of support should include.

Equity means identifying and meeting the needs of all students for academic, behavioral, and social success.

Table 4: Three Tiers of Support in MTSS

MULTI-TIER SYSTEM OF SUPPORT TABLE			
	TIER 1	**TIER 2**	**TIER 3**
	Outcome-Focused Data for School-Wide Decision Making, Curriculum, and Strategies		
TIER SUPPORT LEVELS	• **Designed for 100 percent of all learners** with the target of reaching grade-level expectations for the majority (at least 80 percent) of all students • All students receive high-quality, culturally and linguistically responsive (CLR), standards-based instruction in the classroom setting.	• **Some students, up to 15 percent, not meeting (or exceeding) goals** will receive Tier 2 intervention. • Prescribed level of intensity, duration, and frequency of daily instruction to assist in mastering grade-level content • Educator adjusts instruction for students performing above and below grade-level expectations.	• **Individualized intervention and support designed for a very few students, 3 to 5 percent** • If Tier 1 and 2 supports are not effective, then a few students will need to receive intensive, specifically designed support.
ASSESSMENT TOOLS	School-wide system: Universal screeners, diagnostic, progress monitoring, outcomes evaluation	Diagnostic, progress monitoring with feedback and guidance, outcomes evaluation	Diagnostic, weekly progress monitoring with feedback and guidance, outcomes evaluation
ACADEMIC/ SOCIAL GROUPINGS	**All students and flexible groupings:** Pro-social-emotional curriculum, universal classroom management, clear behavioral goals, progressive discipline, universal behavior screener, restorative justice	**Small groups (4 to 8 students):** Differentiated reinforcement, SEL instruction, behavioral contracts, home/school partnerships, and so on	**Individual (1 to 3 students):** Counseling, assessments, wrap-around services—behavioral intervention plans
WEEKLY TIME ALLOTMENT	**ELA:** • Kinder: 60 minutes per day • 1–5: 90 minutes per day • 6–8: 80 minutes per day **Math:** • Kinder: 30 minutes per day • 1–5: 60 minutes per day • 6–8: 50 minutes per day **SEL:** 15 min per day	**60 additional minutes per week** (3 x 20 minutes or 2 x 30 minutes)	**120–135 additional minutes per week** (3 x 45-minute sessions or 3 x 20 minutes + 2 x 30 minutes)

Tier 1 (100 percent of students): Starting with universal screening tools to identify students at risk and students on track, teams of teachers plan high-quality core instruction and intervention that is culturally and linguistically responsive for the whole class and that should result in 80 percent of students meeting grade-level expectations. Instruction is provided by the classroom teacher and is preventive, proactive, and differentiated using flexible grouping. Innovative leaders prioritize time during regular working hours for collaborative problem-solving, data analysis, utilizing diagnostic and progress monitoring (assessments, student work samples, planning next steps), and making it part of the school culture to foster collective teacher efficacy.

Tier 2 (15 percent of students): Targeted or strategic instruction and intervention are given to some students who are not meeting grade-level goals. Diagnostic and progress-monitoring data are used to guide teachers on how to provide the prescribed level of intensity, frequency, and duration of instruction to support an additional 15 percent of students to master grade-level expectations. Instruction can be provided by the classroom teacher or other available staff in a small-group setting and can include some time with computer-assisted instruction.

Tier 3 (5 percent of students; intensive few): If Tier 1 and 2 supports are not effective, then a few students will need to receive intensive, specifically designed support. Intensive curriculum should be delivered by a specialist in a small-group (one to three students) or individual setting and progress monitoring increases to provide weekly feedback on teaching and learning. This additional support results in another 4 percent of students mastering grade-level expectations.

The Role of Culturally and Linguistically Responsive Instruction in MTSS

What do experts tell us about culturally and linguistically responsive (CLR) instruction and how can we integrate it into multi-tiered system of support? When we look at the first core component as described by the California Department of Education for building a strong response to instruction and intervention system, we see that it clearly states that *every student should receive high-quality, standards-based instruction that is culturally and linguistically responsive in the classroom setting by qualified teachers*. CLR may not be the most important aspect of instruction, but it can be the most impactful, much in the same way baking powder is in cake mix. Just as baking powder enables a cake to rise, CLR instruction allows all students to authentically engage and thrive at school.

Everything in the world around us is culturally and linguistically responsive to someone. The challenge to educators is to match their instruction with the cultural and linguistic needs of the students they serve. Equity means giving each student what they need to be successful at school and in life. CLR is always integrated into the foundation for MTSS models with diverse student populations. "CLR helps us to go where students are culturally and linguistically with the goal of taking them where they need to be academically and socially" (Hollie, 2017).

Geneva Gay and Gloria Ladson-Billings each describe *culturally responsive pedagogy* as encompassing the social-emotional, relational, and cognitive aspects of teaching culturally and linguistically diverse students. Yet, according to Zaretta Hammond, author of *Culturally Responsive Teaching and the Brain: Promoting Authentic Engagement and Rigor Among Culturally and Linguistically Diverse Students* (2014), research around closing the achievement gap for underserved students has not included ways for students to build brain power. For the past 20 years, research has focused on the potential of using cognitive science to boost learning outcomes for all students. Many texts, articles, and educational leaders tout brain-based research, but only a few intentionally integrate brain-based teaching approaches to enhance culturally responsive instruction.

> The challenge to educators is to match their instruction with the cultural and linguistic needs of the students they serve.

Hammond's book can serve as a mentor text on how to operationalize culturally responsive teaching (CRT). Hammond defines CRT as "an educator's ability to recognize students' cultural displays of learning and meaning making and respond positively and constructively with teaching moves that use cultural knowledge as the scaffold to connect what the student knows to new concepts and content in order to promote effective information processing. All the while, the educator understands the importance of being in a relationship and having a social-emotional connection to the students in order to create a safe place for learning" (Hammond, 2014). She cites CRT as one of the most powerful tools for helping students find their way out of the achievement gap and asserts that utilizing a systematic approach to CRT is the perfect catalyst to stimulate the brain to grow brain cells that help us think in more sophisticated ways.

Clearly CRT has the ability to build intellectual capacity. So how do we put it into action? The centerpiece of Hammond's book is the Ready for Rigor framework, which is designed to help educators turn culturally responsive pedagogical principles into culturally responsive teaching practices. The framework is organized around four key areas of teacher capacity building that can set the stage for helping students move from dependent to independent learners, ready to take on rigorous content as they move toward higher education and careers. These four practice areas, which are connected through the principles of brain-based learning, are: awareness, learning partnerships, information processing, and community building. According to Hammond, the tools and strategies from each area need to be blended together to create the social-emotional and cognitive conditions that allow students to engage more actively and take ownership of their learning process. The following is an example of what teachers learn while moving through one of the four practice areas in Hammond's Ready for Rigor framework.

> **Practice Area 3: Information Processing**
>
> Moving through this area, teachers learn how to:
>
> • understand how culture impacts the brain's information processing;
> • orchestrate learning so it builds student's brain power in culturally congruent ways; and
> • use brain-based information-processing strategies common to oral cultures.

Including the "L" in Culturally Responsive Teaching

Culturally and linguistically responsive (CLR) teaching is a holistic approach that recognizes the importance of including student interests and cultural references in all aspects of teaching and learning. Dr. Sharroky Hollie is a national CLR expert, a former principal, university professor, and author of several books, including *Culturally and Linguistically Responsive Teaching and Learning: Classroom Practices for Student* Success (2017). His work emphasizes the importance of validating and affirming the culture and language of our students for the purpose of building and bringing them to success in the culture of academia and mainstream society.

According to Dr. Hollie, "CLR can help educators go where the students are culturally and linguistically, in order to take them where they need to be academically and socially—and should be integrated into the core curriculum and the school culture. It is a framework that can be used to infuse engaging and empowering teaching strategies into diverse classrooms. It is the how and why of teaching and strategic use of methods and instructional decisions to ensure effective teaching and learning for all students."

In order to be a culturally and linguistically responsive educator, it is critical to account for the multiple, overlapping identities within students. Dr. Hollie's work highlights the rings of culture that outline the layered identities, or cultures, that make up who we are. The rings of culture include: ethnicity, sexual orientation, nationality, socioeconomic status, religion, gender, and age (Hollie, 2017). Each of these rings is a potential source of responsiveness for the educator.

While there are a variety of ways to operationalize CLR, the framework developed by Dr. Hollie outlines five pedagogical areas for putting CLR principles into practice:

1. **Academic vocabulary development:** Students have a comprehensive and conceptual knowledge base rooted in their cultural and life experiences that can be used to build and expand academic vocabulary.

2. **Classroom management:** Responsive classroom management validates and affirms students through the use of effective attention signals and protocols that address participation and discussion, infusion of movement, and extended collaboration opportunities. It increases student engagement and decreases off-task behavior.

3. **Academic literacy instruction:** Academic literacy instruction employs culturally authentic and linguistically responsive complex texts to provide more opportunities for students to see themselves in the curriculum.

4. **Academic language instruction:** This is designed to enable students to learn how to move from their home language to the language of school. Teachers understand the nature of nonstandard language and subscribe to a belief system that validates and affirms the use of such language as a vehicle to build and bridge.

5. **Learning environment:** Creating a positive, responsive learning environment takes into consideration both physical factors (elements that make classrooms intellectually stimulating to students) and social factors (fair and clear procedures for behaviors that contribute to a sense of community in the classroom).

Teachers engage with these five areas across the curriculum and throughout the day. By focusing on these five areas, teachers can make critical and positive connections to their students on a consistent basis. When looking at instruction from the *what* and the *how* perspectives, these five areas of CLR can have immediate impact by increasing student motivation and engagement.

Conclusion

High-quality schools differentiate instruction, services, and resource distribution to respond effectively to the diverse needs of their students, with the aim of ensuring that all students are able to learn and thrive. An MTSS framework provides a blueprint for success that clearly lays out the game plan for working with students of varying needs and supports teachers with opportunities to build their students' capacity off of the strength of their colleagues. MTSS can reduce the guesswork and the negative effect of unconscious biases that may deny students the opportunity to reach their full potential.

There is no shortcut for meeting the needs of all students, and it requires developing the mindset and the skillset of both educators and students. It requires support and teamwork from administration and co-teachers and the scheduling of space and time for planning and evaluating with other team members during the school day. To have collective teacher buy-in, educators must be fully informed on the research that supports MTSS (i.e., RTI[2], CLR, PBIS). These systematic approaches help remove emotions, unconscious biases, guesswork, and good intentions (e.g., rescue syndrome, missionaries, ego, exclusivity) to ensure success for all students. The learning curve will vary based on teachers' experience, commitment, and efficacy and will require professional development. MTSS challenges all educators to develop more sophisticated classroom management skills to move from a traditional model to a more student-focused classroom. It may require budget adjustments for training and the purchase of computer-assisted programs, pro-social-emotional curriculum, culturally empowering classroom libraries, and other resources. The training will need to be extended to the whole school community, including counselors, psychologists, resource teachers, as well as parents, for all students to achieve equity in the classroom.

Building equity is the behavior of people who care. Be the change.

Kandice McLurkin, M.Ed., has over 39 years of experience creating and leading professional development for teachers, administrators, university partners, and community leaders on promoting equity in the educational setting with a strong emphasis on collective teacher efficacy, culturally responsive pedagogy, and fostering resiliency. Under her leadership, UCLA identified LAUSD's Academic English Mastery Program (AEMP) as a national model in educator training and resource development that prepares educators to use culturally responsive teaching and implement academic language development instruction to help close achievement gaps for culturally and linguistically diverse students. A former LAUSD central office administrator and elementary school principal in the historic Los Angeles community of West Adams, McLurkin was especially successful with serving African American, Latine, and all underserved students, as evidenced by outstanding standardized testing data. McLurkin has worked with universities, professional organizations, and all stakeholders to embrace the research and evidence-based resources that help all students thrive. She is the cofounder and CEO of Rose Equity Collective.

Seeing and Teaching the Whole Child

by Fay E. Brown, Ph.D.

As an educational consultant, I spend much of my time working with school leaders to institute changes in programs, policies, and procedures to improve conditions for students and the broader school community. I often attend meetings that serve as an opportunity to deepen my understanding of school functioning and as a mechanism to provide coaching and feedback to the administrators and staff on various issues.

In a meeting I attended in 2018, a teacher made some comments that deeply affected me. Near the end of our meeting, she said to the administrative intern who was sitting in for the principal, "Of all the years I have been a teacher, this has been my most challenging year. Mrs. Waters (pseudonym), we need to talk to the principal about what we as a school should do about students who can't learn, students who are incapable of learning, who come to school to infringe on the civil rights of other students."

I was stunned to hear a teacher describe students in that manner, and I didn't want the meeting to end and everyone to disperse without at least asking her for some clarification. In the most "no-fault" tone that I was able to manage at that moment, I asked her if she had intended to describe the students as "can't learn and incapable of learning." We hadn't met before, so she didn't know who I was. She had also joined the meeting a few minutes late, so she had missed the part when we introduced ourselves at the beginning. This teacher responded, "If you understand how the brain works, you would know that there are some children who just can't learn." Wow! I gently reminded her and the rest of the group that "every child who comes through the schoolhouse door can learn. What each child learns and the rate at which he/she learns might vary, but *every child can learn*."

After the meeting, the chairperson met with me for a few minutes and explained that she was taken aback by the teacher's comments because she knows her to be one of the best teachers in the school. When I drove out of the school's parking lot that morning, tears rolled down my cheeks as I thought about the teacher's words and their implications for those students in her class whom she identified as "can't learn and incapable of learning." I needed to process my thoughts and feelings with somebody, so I called my friend and former colleague Dr. Christine Emmons, who lived about seven minutes away. We spent the next hour or so analyzing and dissecting the teacher's words and situating them within the context of the Child Development Mindset Theory of Change model we had created a few years previously for our organization, the School Development Program.

In that model, we assert that a teacher with a child development mindset believes that the focus of education is the development of the student, and that development and learning are inextricably linked. Further, we assert that such a teacher has the attitude that his or her job is to facilitate the holistic development of each child and understands that:

- students go through stages of development, but development is uneven;

Teaching with a child development mindset means making sure every student experiences some success every day.

- development activities and experiences should be integrated into the curriculum and instruction; and

- positive relationships are critical for the nurturing of student development and learning.

We posit that this mindset is manifested through teachers' understandings, attitudes, and behaviors, which are translated into a development-focused classroom. Such a classroom is characterized by management and instructional strategies based on child development principles. This results in improved student attitudes toward school and learning, improved student behavior, increased student motivation and resilience, and increased academic achievement.

Equity and a Developmental Mindset

The greater part of my work focuses on helping educators understand that a developmental understanding is the foundation of education. Recently, I started thinking that the concept of equity in the classroom can be reimagined and considered from the perspective of that developmental understanding. More specifically, when *equity* is defined as "meeting the needs of each child to ensure success," the chance of garnering that success increases when we approach fulfilling those needs from a holistic perspective, using the Six Developmental Pathways framework of the Comer model. These pathways are physical, cognitive, language, social, ethical, and psychological. (See Table 5 on page 48 for a detailed description of each pathway.)

The central premise of this developmental, holistic perspective is that a student's success in school is not merely contingent upon what he or she is capable of doing cognitively, but that the other pathways are as relevant and as important to his or her success. These pathways are interconnected; thus, underdevelopment or disruption along one pathway can have a significant impact on other pathways, especially the cognitive. For example, McGonigal (2014) noted that "when you are experiencing shame or being let down, the prefrontal cortex is as impacted as when you are sleep deprived." Insufficient sleep is linked to reduced short-term memory and learning ability, negative mood, inconsistent performance, poor productivity, and loss of some form of behavior control, according to researchers from the National Institutes of Health (Eugene & Masiak, 2015). So, if the teacher from the beginning of this essay demonstrated attitudes and behaviors that sent her students the message that they can't learn and are incapable of learning, then there is a strong probability that her attitudes and behaviors toward those students were major contributors to their underachievement.

Table 5: The Six Developmental Pathways

PATHWAYS	DESCRIPTION
Physical	The physical pathway refers to the physical health and well-being of children. In addressing this pathway, the goal is to help children and adolescents acquire knowledge about their physical development and to use this knowledge to make good decisions that will promote healthy development.
Cognitive	The cognitive pathway refers to an individual's ability to think critically and creatively, to retain and mentally manipulate information, and to set and work toward accomplishing desired goals. In addressing this pathway, the goal is for children and adolescents to increase their capacity to analyze, synthesize, and evaluate information; to achieve mastery in required and selected content areas; to use information to solve problems effectively; and to enjoy learning.
Language	This pathway refers to: a) receptive language, which is an individual's ability to understand spoken and written communication and to accurately interpret nonverbal cues; and b) expressive language, the ability to communicate effectively, both verbally and through writing. In addressing this pathway, the goal is to help children and adolescents increase their capacity for receptive and expressive language in a variety of contexts.
Social	This pathway refers to the individual's ability to develop and maintain healthy relationships and to adequately negotiate challenging relationships. In addressing this pathway, the goal is to help children and adolescents increase their capacity to build and maintain healthy relationships across the range of human diversity.
Ethical	The ethical pathway focuses on the individual's knowledge of appropriate and acceptable behaviors as well as the practice of these behaviors, including respect for the rights and integrity of self and others. In addressing this pathway, the goal is to help children and adolescents increase their capacity to behave with justice and fairness toward others and enhance their ability to make decisions that promote their well-being and the collective good.
Psychological	This pathway focuses on an individual's self-awareness and self-esteem, including feelings of worth and competence. It also refers to an individual's ability to manage emotions appropriately. The goals in addressing this pathway are to help children and adolescents develop a strong, positive sense of self and to increase their capacity to manage their emotions well.

Brown, F., Emmons, C., & Joyner, E. (2006).
School Development Program; Yale Child Study Center

Teachers who demonstrate that developmental understanding report an actualization of that development-focused classroom articulated in our Theory of Change model. Consider the following two observations. The first is from Christina Natale, a first-year teacher who had attended our developmental pathways training a couple months before she started teaching. Natale explains:

> The academy for me was truly eye-opening. I learned so much. But what I learned became really important once I was in the real-life setting of the classroom. The Six Developmental Pathways became everything for me. Every day when kids come up to me upset, it's as if I automatically go over the pathways in my head, and I find myself thinking: "Are you hungry? Are you sad? What might really be going on behind your being upset?"
>
> Actually, I had a really emotional group of students in that class, and I found that the pathways understanding really impacted how I interacted with them. I am not saying it was easy, because it wasn't. But when they acted out, I found myself thinking that "this is not *who* they are, it's *how* they are acting. They can come out of it." I take into consideration what they are dealing with; not just cognitively, but physically, psychologically, and along all the other pathways. Using that thinking and strategies along the pathways helps my school day go by a lot smoother. Had I not attended that academy and learned about the Developmental Pathways and the importance of relationships in the classroom, my first year of teaching would have been a lot more difficult (Christina Natale, one-on-one interview, 2017).

The second teacher, Larissa Giordano, is a more experienced teacher who had attended different training events with us and received onsite classroom support. Giordano is a teacher in the New Haven Public School System with whom I have had the pleasure of working for several years. In 2012, we published an article in *The Handbook of Prosocial Education* in which she provided several examples of how she expertly integrated the six developmental pathways into her curriculum, instruction, and assessment and in her daily interactions with her fourth-grade students. In particular, she explained the significantly positive outcomes for students when they understand themselves through the lens of those pathways, including when they reflect in their Pathways Journal. She included the following story:

> One morning, while entering the classroom, I could tell right away that something was bothering Allejah. I thought it might be a good idea to make a quick change to my lesson plan and allow for five minutes of reflection in the Pathways Journals. As I circled the room, I peeked at Allejah's entry in the "Please Help

Me" section and noticed her eyes welling up with tears as she wrote. She was writing about needing help with her psychological pathway. I asked her to join me outside for a quick talk. She shared with me that she had an argument with her mom that morning and was feeling upset about how she left it, as she jumped out of the car for school, slamming the door behind her. Tearfully she told me she was afraid her mom didn't know that she was sorry and that she loved her. Feeling empathy for Allejah and knowing how her state of mind might impact the rest of her day, I allowed her to use the phone to call her mom. I connected her with her mom and allowed her two minutes for her conversation. She returned to the classroom with a smile and whispered "thank you" to me as she passed. Having resolved that issue, I knew she was ready to start the day (Comer et al., 2012).

This story from Giordano underscores an important conceptualization of equity recently made by the renowned educator Dr. Edmund Gordon. To commemorate his 100th birthday, faculty and friends from Teachers College, Columbia University, convened a virtual two-day centennial conference in May 2021 to honor him. Among Dr. Gordon's scholarly work is his emphasis on equity in education. In his closing comments, he made a distinction between equality and equity in education. He stated, "Equal suggests sameness. But, for educational opportunities to be equal, they shouldn't be the same but should be customized." In other words, they should be equitable. He added, "You figure out what each learner needs, and you customize."

Giordano's story about Allejah is illustrative of that customizing mentioned by Dr. Gordon. Giordano noticed that the student had a particular need that was not about her intellectual capacity but nevertheless could affect her academic performance and even her behavior throughout the day had she not paused to give attention to that need. Giordano's reflection shows how having that developmental mindset allows for a consistent assessment and interpretation of students' behavior based on their developmental need at the time and the teacher's sincere attempt to respond to those needs—in other words, figuring out what each learner needs and customizing. I could include many more scenarios from teachers; however, the salient point being emphasized is that a teacher with a child development mindset is a teacher who will demonstrate equity in the classroom. Giordano summed up her experiences that year as follows:

> Although this was not my first year teaching, it was my first year teaching at this school, and I felt it was my best and most productive year as a teacher. . . . Although there is always room for growth, I felt satisfied with how I was teaching and with how the students were learning. . . . I learned that trust thrives only when the students know the teacher is on their side; that when

the students know they are cared for, they believe in themselves and want to live up to the expectations they have for themselves, as well as those set by the teacher. . . . I knew that although the students change and their needs change, the developmental principles remain the same. Thus, the focus did not need to be on a particular management method, but on finding ways to support the development of each student (Comer et al., 2012).

Customizing to Meet Students' Needs: The Essentials of Literacy Program

The idea of customizing to meet the needs of the learner brings to mind a reading program implemented by the School Development Program for several years. During my first ten years on this job, I spent a significant portion of my time collaborating with Dr. Edward T. Murray, a professor at Sacred Heart University in Bridgeport, Connecticut, to develop and implement an elementary-level reading intervention program called the Essentials of Literacy (EOL). This program brings together the child-centered strategies of the Comer process with research-based instructional strategies to improve the literacy skills of struggling elementary level students. EOL consists of small-group instruction carried out at literacy stations—story, phonics, guided reading, vocabulary, writing, and listening—among which students rotate at 20-minute intervals. Each station is facilitated by a caring adult, includes a wide range of engaging materials, and involves frequent assessment to monitor students' progress. These stations are set up in a "Reading Room," which is described as:

- a classroom in which adults demonstrate the belief that all children can learn.

- a classroom where students read, write, listen, think, learn, and make good decisions for at least 90 minutes each day.

- a classroom where students who are experiencing difficulty with their reading skills learn to become good readers in a highly stimulating, nurturing environment.

- a classroom where students experience success on a daily basis and celebrate their successes at the end of each week.

- a classroom where members of the community assist a teacher in promoting students' mastery of the language arts, while helping to facilitate other aspects of their development.

- a classroom where child development theories and principles undergird the daily practices and activities (Brown & Murray, 2005).

The guiding principles of the Reading Room epitomize the definition of equity in the classroom used in this essay, i.e., providing for the needs of each learner to ensure his or her success. They also fit Dr. Gordon's goals of figuring out what each learner needs and customizing to meet those needs. The above description of the Reading Room includes a reference to students experiencing success. During the training provided for all Reading Room staff, I laid out what I referred to as "a non-negotiable expectation" of the program: **Every day, every student *must* experience some success.** That expectation became the EOL motto for everyone, and each station facilitator worked to make that expectation a reality.

One example of achieving that success is frequently demonstrated at the writing station. Often, there would be at least one student in each rotating group of four who would assert that he or she can't write the story assignment based on the theme for that week. To ensure that the student turns the "I can't" into "I will try"—and, in doing so, experience some success—the station facilitator would do the following:

1. Have the student verbally share something he or she would write on the topic.

2. Write the student's sentence on a sentence strip.

3. Cut the strip into meaningful parts and shuffle the parts to separate them.

4. Ask the student to put the parts back together to create the sentence.

The facilitator would then ask the student to copy that sentence from the sentence strip into his or her own writing book. That activity moves the student away from "I can't write" to actually writing a complete statement on a particular topic. Students' "I can't" is not based on a physical incapability to hold a pencil to do the writing, but on a psychological fear of not knowing what to write or messing up trying to spell the words as they attempt to write. By having the student articulate the sentence and following the above sequence, those barriers are removed, and the student experiences success in writing at least one sentence during that rotation.

The activities executed daily at each station allow for every student to experience some degree of success regardless of his or her level of reading. Let's consider another station—the vocabulary station. Every day, each student is encouraged to learn five new words and to add these words to his or her vocabulary book. Although the expectation is five new words, if a student learns one or two new words in a day, that is considered success because he or she still increases her repertoire of words on a daily basis. This learning takes place in a classroom where positive relationships serve as a foundation for the interactions between adults and students and among the students.

It's important to point out that students who are selected to spend that language arts block in the Reading Room are often reading two to three levels below their grade level. The program is implemented at third grade, and most of the students chosen to participate were reading on kindergarten to first-grade levels. Many of them are also identified by their teachers as having behavior problems. However, with this intense focus on ameliorating those reading challenges within a classroom of caring adults who demonstrate positive relationships toward every child and encourage and reward incremental successes, every student improves greatly, making a year-and-a-half to two years' gain in their reading within eight months.

A student who experiences difficulty with reading can become a good reader in a highly stimulating, nurturing environment.

Speaking of students making improvements, one particular story comes to mind. Each year, my colleagues and I convene for a week of professional development for teachers called the Academy for Developmentally Centered Education. This week of training is held at a hotel in New Haven, Connecticut, with about 270 teachers from Comer schools across the country in attendance. During this training, I invite students from a couple of New Haven schools to join us for a panel discussion to share with those teachers some of the factors that both promote and impede students' learning. One year, a student who had recently exited the EOL program was a member the panel. I also invited his classroom teacher, Shelia Brantley, to co-facilitate the discussion with me.

At one point in the discussion, Mrs. Brantley said to the student, "Sean (pseudonym), tell Dr. Brown the kind of student you were before you started going to the EOL Reading Room." He looked at me and said, "I was a bad student. I acted out a lot." Wow, to hear a student describe himself in those words! I asked him, "What caused you to act out a lot?" He responded, "I acted out because I couldn't read. The other students could read, and I couldn't, so I felt sad and acted out." I thought, "What a profound statement from a fourth grader!" Mrs. Brantley then said to him, "Tell Dr. Brown the kind of student you are now." With a smile that could completely light up a darkened room, Sean looked at me and at the audience and said, "I can read now, so I no longer act out. I behave myself now." An applause erupted from the audience, sparing them from seeing my tears falling down my cheeks.

Over the years as I conduct workshops with teachers, I share with them one "Fay Brownism" to keep in mind: "Often, children behave the way they feel. If they are feeling good or happy, you will see it in their behavior. And, if they are feeling bad or sad, you will see it in their behavior." Sean confirmed that philosophy. His experience and statements highlight the need for teachers to have that developmental mindset and take a holistic approach in working with students. His feelings (the psychological pathway) greatly impacted his behaviors (social and physical pathways), which were greatly impacted by his inability to read and achieve academically (cognitive pathway). But he had teachers who did not give up on him, who customized the learning experience to meet his needs.

There are many, many students like Sean across this country who are placed in classrooms with teachers like the one first referenced in this essay; students who, due to no fault of their own, are in jeopardy of being on a trajectory of failure. But that trajectory can be changed when equity is actualized in the classroom through programs like EOL and with teachers like Christina Natale, Larissa Giordano, and Shelia Brantley, who expertly infuse a developmental understanding in their classroom practices and are consistently mindful of the importance of the teacher-student relationship for positive student outcomes.

The Importance of Relationships in the Classroom

Children's development is contingent on positive relationships with the adults around them. Since I have postulated that development is the foundation of education, then positive relationships between teacher and students are central to students' learning. Helping teachers understand the importance of those relationships for effective classroom function has been one of my key areas of focus for professional development sessions.

One of the modules I do with teachers is designed to help them examine their relationship with each student in their class. I have them start by writing the names of every student in their classroom, then provide them with specific areas on which to focus. For example:

- Put a check mark beside the names of the students on whom you call most often to respond to content/lesson-related questions.
- Put a minus sign beside the names of the students you tend to give up on quickly and move on to someone else when you ask those questions.

- Put an X beside the names of the students who are presenting some behavior challenges to you so far this academic year or the students on whom you often call out for behavior-related issues.
- Put a plus sign beside the names of the students you consider your favorites.

These are four of about seven specific dimensions on which I ask teachers to reflect. I then ask them to look for correlations among the dimensions in terms of the students whose names appear in overlapping areas and see if there are surprises or if certain patterns emerge. The discussion that ensues is invariably eye-opening and a change-leveraging step for several teachers.

One of the objectives of this activity is to help teachers understand that sometimes student behavior in the classroom is precipitated by teacher attitudes and behaviors. Sometimes, teachers are seemingly not conscious of expressing some of those attitudes toward students. Further, the activity helps to underscore that teacher behavior, including expressions of high or low expectations, can either foster or impede positive relationships in the classroom and can lead to favorable or unfavorable outcomes for students and teachers.

> Sometimes student behavior in the classroom is precipitated by teacher attitudes and behavior. Sometimes, teachers are seemingly not conscious of expressing some of those attitudes toward students.

A couple of months after conducting this session in one school, I returned to meet with the administrator and a few teachers to learn their perspectives on the impact of the work being done in the school. A fourth-grade teacher shared that as a result of her self-examination done during that professional development session, she decided to bring the activity to her class the following day and engage her students in a similar analysis and discussion.

She explained to her students that she wanted to get their honest feedback about how they experience her treatment of them so that she can learn from them about any changes she might need to make to help improve the culture and climate of the class. She asked her class if there were students whom she seems to call on consistently to answer questions, whom she seems to ignore and never calls on, whom she seems to call on only regarding behavior issues, and whom she tends to treat like they were her favorites. She shared with us that she was surprised and humbled by the honesty and openness of many children in her classroom. They named several students whom they believe fell in each category. Some revelations surprised and delighted her, while others required her to apologize openly to some students. The overall result was a more positive classroom climate and closer relationships between her and several students.

In her TED Talk video, "Every Kid Needs a Champion," the late Rita Pierson quoted the leader of our School Development Program, James P. Comer, saying, "No significant learning can occur without a significant relationship."

In describing some of the students she taught over the years, she said, "I have had classes that were so low; so academically deficient that I cried. I wondered, 'How am I going to take this group in nine months from where they are to where they need to be? . . . How do I raise the self-esteem of a child and his academic achievement at the same time?'" (2013).

Pierson goes on to describe how she talked to the students to help them see themselves in a positive manner, telling them how special they were and even how they need to carry themselves even as they walk along the hallways. In addition, she taught them the following affirmation that she repeated with them daily:

> "I am somebody. I was somebody when I came; I will be a better somebody when I leave. I am powerful and I am strong. I deserve the education that I get here. I have things to do, people to impress, and places to go."

She added, "You say it long enough, it starts to be part of you."

Pierson demonstrated what Carol Dweck and colleagues refer to as a growth mindset toward her students. She understood the "yet factor" about teaching and about growth and development: That is, just because a student doesn't know something now doesn't mean that he or she won't know it at some point. It just means that the student doesn't know it *yet*. If a teacher has a growth mindset (which is the same as the developmental mindset described earlier in this chapter), he or she will have that understanding and the attitude that his or her job is to facilitate the student's learning of whatever that concept or that lesson might be. In her book *Mindset*, Dweck explains that a teacher with a growth mindset does not just pay lip service to the idea that all children can learn but has "a deep desire to reach in and ignite the mind of every child." She adds, "Growth mindset teachers ask: 'How can I teach them?' not 'Can I teach them?' And, 'How will they learn?' not 'Can they learn?'" (Dweck, 2007).

Summary

Those questions asked by growth mindset teachers embody what Rita Pierson described about her mindset for her students, and they are evident in the scenarios described by Larissa Giordano and Christina Natale. In other words, reimagining equity in the classroom is contingent on teachers having and demonstrating a developmental or growth mindset toward their students, believing in the possibilities and potentials of each student, and operationalizing that mindset through programs and strategies aimed at meeting the needs of every student.

For teachers to have and demonstrate those qualities, many of them need support, including professional development that is not only content-related, to help improve their instructional practices, but also the kind that can inspire and challenge them to be their best and to see and cultivate the best in every student. Every year at the end of our academy, teachers complete a reflection sheet about their experience of the week. The comments are generally overwhelmingly positive, but one particular comment at the end of our 2019 academy impacted me greatly and left me wishing that every teacher who is experiencing a year like the one described by the teacher at the beginning of this essay could have a similar experience. This teacher wrote:

> Honestly, I entered this training with no expectations because this was my first one. Some of the materials that were taught were not new because I learned them in college. However, the way that they were delivered at this training was amazing. After a truly devastating year that I feared would jade me, this training fueled my pedagogical soul. It reversed my negative mindset. Thank you! I am excited for the new school year.

Fay E. Brown, Ph.D., an associate research scientist at the Child Study Center at Yale University, serves as the director of child and adolescent development for the School Development Program in the Center. Dr. Brown has worked at the elementary, high school, and college levels, teaching and counseling students. Her major focus in her current position is to help schools create and maintain developmentally appropriate conditions to ensure the holistic development of every child. Dr. Brown has authored and co-authored journal articles about the reading achievement of struggling elementary school students and about the over-representation of African American students in special education classes. She has also co-authored chapters in such books as *Six Pathways to Healthy Child Development and Academic Success* and *Dynamic Instructional Leadership to Support Student Learning and Development*. Dr. Brown has served as an educational consultant to individual schools, school districts, and various other groups, including parent groups. She serves on a number of boards and committees, including Connecticut Employment and Training Commission's (CETC) Adult Literacy Leadership Board; Scholastic's National Advisory Council; Yale-Scholastic Collaborative for Child and Family Resilience; and the Nathan Ebanks Foundation in Kingston, Jamaica.

Promoting High Student Achievement

by Robert L. Green, Ph.D.

> **"I have the audacity to believe that people everywhere can have three meals a day for their bodies, education and culture for their minds, and dignity, equality, and freedom for their spirits."**
> —DR. MARTIN LUTHER KING, JR.

As an education consultant for public school districts, I visit schools on a regular basis. When students and teachers learn that I worked with Dr. Martin Luther King, Jr., they are amazed. One elementary student asked, "You knew Dr. Martin Luther King, Jr.?" He then added, "You must be really old."

I asked him, "How old do you think I am?"

He said, "About 200!"

While I am not 200, I am old enough to have seen the progress made toward educational equity since the early days of the Civil Rights Movement, and I am experienced enough to see the work that must still be done to promote high student achievement among *all* students.

Dr. King said many times that education was one of the most important factors related to liberation. He finished high school when he was 15 years old. He graduated from Morehouse College at the age of 19 with a Bachelor of Arts in sociology. He was 26 when he received his Ph.D. in philosophy. Because he believed strongly in the importance of education, Dr. King worked with

Thurgood Marshall and others to promote education at the community level throughout the country.

Today, many factors and real barriers to learning can affect the academic performance of students. These include indifference, rejection, poor instruction, and low expectations for student success. The expectations teachers have for their students' academic outcome influence the way the students view themselves (Green, 2009). How students view themselves affects their own expectations, and this has an impact on their academic performance (Stearns, 2017). How might teachers increase the opportunities for students to embrace academics each day and help students cultivate and nurture a positive viewpoint of themselves? In this essay, I share some of my personal experiences from my years helping students build a positive identity as learners, leading to high academic achievement.

Hold High Expectations for Student Achievement

I was an educational consultant at an elementary school in Las Vegas. During a break in a tenth-grade class, some boys came out of the classroom. One of the boys was being a little aggressive, laughing, and having fun. His teacher said, "If you're not careful, you'll end up just like your daddy . . . in prison!"

When I heard that, my heart sank. I told the boys to go on to class, then said to the teacher, "That was a terrible thing to say to this young person. You are creating a negative mindset that could create a potential negative course of action, just because of a little pushy behavior. You're holding low expectations."

I was going to go to the principal but chose not to. Instead, I followed up with the teacher and sat in on her class. She eventually shared with me that she didn't mean to indicate that the boy was going to end up in prison, even though that was what she said. She explained that she was trying to scare him into doing the right thing.

"But you're not scaring him into doing the right thing," I said. "You are setting him on a path of expectations that might end up leading to behaviors that could result in the outcome you presented."

What are expectations? They are a belief system by which we abide to elicit behaviors from those we want to succeed. They are a belief system that becomes a philosophy of life: the way we live, the way we treat people, and in any school setting, the way we treat our students.

Expectations are very important in terms of helping young people adjust and succeed in school. Success is related to how we treat our students. When students understand that they are expected to perform poorly, they have a more difficult time succeeding. Teachers must be respectful and responsive toward

> **Teachers with high expectations will work to ensure that students achieve those standards using a variety of methods and strategies.**

every student, regardless of the student's income, race, ethnicity, religion, disability, sexual orientation and gender identity, and culture. Teachers who hold high expectations for all students are respectful of diversity. They do not judge or discriminate against students and are aware that they may not know what a student's circumstances might be, but they do understand that all students are capable of learning. They trust that every student is a capable learner and may not learn at the same rate as others. Teachers with high expectations will work to ensure that students achieve those standards using a variety of methods and strategies.

Offer Each Student Academic Prosperity

Some students are in situations at home that are neither pleasant nor comfortable. Teachers need to know how to recognize when a student needs the help of a school counselor, social worker, or psychologist. Is there a parent, relative, or sibling taking care of the student? Is the home climate positive, safe, and nurturing, or is it dysfunctional? Is hunger an issue? Is there evidence of abuse? It is important to reassure all students that they matter and will be guided to excel academically, regardless of their history, socioeconomic status, culture, or home environment.

Teachers must be particularly mindful of any student living in poverty since it may affect the student's academic performance. Learning cannot take place if a student is hungry. Signs a student is hungry may not be obvious; however, an observant teacher may notice a student misbehave or act withdrawn. In such cases, the teacher should talk privately with the student to determine the cause of the behavior. If hunger is revealed to be the cause of the student's behavior, efforts should be made to connect the student with federally funded programs that may provide food for the evenings and weekends.

We want all children to be able to move away from feeling ashamed of being poor to possessing feelings of strong self-worth, eventually helping them to overcome fear and trauma. Basically, we need to help ensure that children living in poverty are seen as neat, clean, and academically ready to be successful students. The ways students look and present themselves make a difference in terms of peer acceptance. The entire school administration and faculty need to understand and realize that no matter how poor a child is, he or she needs to be seen as a worthy human being. Otherwise, they may make bad judgments regarding the child that could hinder the child's progress at the elementary, middle, and high school levels, and later, on the job and in life. We should always strive to change the student's status from poverty to academic prosperity.

Manage a Classroom That Promotes Student Achievement

Order in the classroom is very important. And when I say order, I don't mean police-type order. I mean structuring a calm, relaxed, but firm classroom. Children need to know that you have control over the classroom in order for them to feel safe and to keep their attention. In my classroom, there was no tug-of-war. We settled things verbally, and students respected me as the instructional leader.

Good classroom management promotes learning. Students will not be able to learn to read in a classroom where confusion, negativity, unsafe conditions, anger, or hostility is present. A classroom must be a safe, nonjudgmental, and civilized space.

How can teachers achieve effective classroom management?

- Create an overall atmosphere (verbal and nonverbal) of general encouragement and support for the learning process of all students.
- Maintain an orderly environment that is safe, structured, and comfortable.
- Have high expectations and set clear standards of attainable academic and behavioral performance.
- Carefully think, plan, and make decisions to ensure strategic teaching.
- Give students adequate time to formulate answers when called upon.
- React to student responses with praise at the appropriate time and in the appropriate amount.

A positive classroom atmosphere promotes learning.

- Use significant amounts of positive, nonverbal behavior, such as smiling, nodding positively, looking students directly in the eye, leaning forward, and encouraging more than one direct response.
- Design learning activities to be challenging, engaging, relevant, and directed to student motivations.
- Place primary stress on academic achievement and do not settle for solely social or other nonacademic goals, such as success in school athletics.
- See the good in each student and expect excellence.
- Help struggling students develop good work habits.

Cultivate Relationships With Families and Caregivers

Research makes clear the pivotal role of family engagement on academic achievement (Henderson et al., 2007; Redding et al., 2011; Scholastic FACE, 2013). There are plenty of ways to get families and caregivers engaged and involved in what is happening in the school. My most recent experience was at an elementary school. The principal wanted to get parents to support a reading program. She decided to start serving a meal to the caregivers who attended the discussion held at the school. She had great food and made sure that the meals ended with delicious homemade desserts, such as pound cake.

I always made a big deal about it in meetings. I said, "We're going to have a good work session tonight. And after that, we're going to have some pound cake that is baking as I speak." The smell of freshly baked cakes wafted out of the kitchen at that elementary school. Families looked forward to attending the school meetings because they felt included and cared for. By creating a welcoming space, the principal encouraged family engagement in the school.

One of the best topics to engage families with is literacy. It is also a critical issue because the most important factor determining student success in school is a child's ability to read (Horbec, 2012).

Here are a few ideas for engaging families in literacy:

- Begin literacy training early in your school district.
- Promote literacy at the middle and high school levels when needed.
- Share the impact of high expectations with parents/caregivers, since often this group has the most influence on how students view themselves.
- Involve community groups in literacy efforts.
- Establish literacy programs for adults who have limited reading skills.

There is no magic formula for helping each learner achieve academic success. It takes creativity, along with a willingness to work hard, be an advocate, and possess concern and love for students and a desire for them to succeed. If we work together, we can help realize my friend Dr. King's dream of an equitable world where all children can succeed, regardless of their skin color, home life, or economic circumstance.

> Helping each learner achieve academic success takes creativity, along with a willingness to work hard, be an advocate, and possess concern and love for students and a desire for them to succeed.

Robert L. Green, Ph.D., holds a doctorate degree in educational psychology from Michigan State University (MSU) and BA and MA from San Francisco State College. He is a former president of the University of the District of Columbia and former dean of the College of Urban Development at Michigan State University. Dr. Green worked for Dr. Martin Luther King, Jr., as the education director of the Southern Christian Leadership Conference from 1965 to 1967. Dr. Green has successfully utilized his writing and research to help solve some of society's most pressing social, political, economic, and racial issues. His research and practice have focused on the impact of poverty and discrimination on urban minority populations. He is a national and international expert on expectations and how they affect student achievement. Dr. Green is dean and professor emeritus and distinguished alumnus of Michigan State University. He and his wife, Lettie, have three sons, R. Vincent Green, J.D.; Kurt Green, M.B.A.; and Kevin Green, Ph.D. Currently, he and his wife reside in Virginia.

Recognizing and Erasing Classroom Inequity

by Alonzo Westbrook

It's Teacher Appreciation Week 2021. Instead of formal professional development, our assistant principal (AP) has decided to celebrate teachers under her supervision by having "fun." It's a virtual celebration. Everyone chimes in remotely. The facilitator of equity at our school, a young Black male hired by our principal, assists the AP, an older White female. The two begin by listing the names of the teachers in our math department on a blackboard. They instruct us: The first teacher chooses a name from the board and says something "nice" about that person. That teacher, in turn, will choose another name, and so on. It's a feel-good session tinged with anticipation and excitement, as well as pressure to speak. It never crossed my mind that anyone wouldn't be picked, but there sat my name at the top of the board, by itself. The third-to-last person, a Millennial White male, chose the older, heavy-accented Eastern European female in our department whose name he hadn't bothered to learn how to pronounce; neither is new to the school. She, in turn, didn't select me but acknowledged everyone for being "great." To close, the AP thanked teachers for their participation. As people began their goodbyes, the facilitator of equity interrupted and said, "Hey, hey, everyone. Before we go, I also want to acknowledge Mr. Westbrook and thank him for helping our school community think outside the box."

I felt—rather, my colleagues made me feel—like an outcast.

Sliding into this odious lesson without a safety net, I had questions. Did the planners, my AP and the facilitator of equity, consider how the last person on the board might feel, or did their idea of "fun" outweigh considerations of equity? Without knowing why—why the facilitators chose to conduct this biased activity and why my colleagues chose not to celebrate my hard work and dedication as a teacher—I rationalized: *They don't like me*. It's reductive, but that's how defenses work. Stuck in that feeling, seeking and needing restoration, I began to justify it.

Professionally, I am among the few of the 82 teachers in my school whom our administration has ever rated highly effective (one out of three in the math department). So, the disregard felt personal, not unlike intimate terrorism— violence used by an abusive person to gain control over another person (Johnson, 2008). As a humanitarian Black male, I have been vocal in my high school about inequity (e.g., the principal locking all bathrooms in a school with a population of over 1,300, and students having to find an adult with a key to open one, resulting in an upperclassman defecating on himself; or locking late students outside of the school building until the start of their next class, even in winter). Our school's principal and most of the school's administrators

Teach students how to set goals and meet them to help them succeed in school and in life.

and teachers are White or Latine, who expressly identify as White or benefit similarly from the protections, opportunities, and advantages of appearing White. Ninety-eight percent of our students are of color. The conversations among staff surrounding equity have been uncomfortable, with troublesome pushback: "What's all the fuss about?" My concern, then as now, was for our students.

Within minutes of signing off from the teacher celebration, I emailed my AP to express my concern that one of the participating teachers might repeat the psychosocially harmful activity in his or her classroom. Two business days went by before she responded. She began by saying she had needed time to figure out what to say to me. She told me she felt bad for me and didn't think through the activity and didn't anticipate the outcome, though she said she'd seen her co-facilitator do it in his classroom. He's under her supervision in the science department. She told me, "To get students talking to one another, in line with the Danielson (teacher observation) rubric, he had one student call on another to verbally share or build upon the other's thinking." I explained the differences between the popcorn activities and how what she and the facilitator did for teacher appreciation created isolation. I suggested they could have given numbers to teachers to make it random. Finally, she said she understood.

> **Does the discomfort that surrounds equity make it too uncomfortable for those not directly impacted by its damaging effects to care enough to dare broach it?**

I expected my AP to use the power of correction within an educator's arsenal to tell the department, via email or at the next meeting, about the inequity that occurred during the celebration activity, so teachers who might use it would be aware of its pitfalls. She didn't. Did she care more about checking off a box for Danielson than about preventing students from being isolated by a teacher practice? Or does the discomfort that surrounds equity make it too uncomfortable for those not directly impacted by its damaging effects to care enough to dare broach it?

Certainly, teachers and administrators have the privilege to turn a blind eye, but therein lies the problem. Educator activities, formal in-school policies (such as bathroom use and attendance), and zero-tolerance behavioral policies for K–12 students still discovering their triggers are rife with inequity. Recognizing inequity depends on the lens through which an educator views and then rationalizes it. Social schema—such as occupation, age, race, religion, gender, sexuality, knowledge, values, beliefs, and assumptions—influence educator responses (what they hear and see) and how they react (often based on whom it affects). Thus, well-intentioned educators can be influenced by certain beliefs and insufficient understandings, which can lead them to behave unjustly toward staff and students alike.

"You'll Never Amount to Nothin'."

In "Juicy," the first single from his debut album *Ready to Die*, the global hip-hop cultural narrator Christopher Wallace, a.k.a. Biggie Smalls, raps about how he dropped out of school because he was a "misunderstood" Black male. He dedicated his first album "to all the teachers that told me I'd never amount to nothin'" (1994). Biggie's voice reflects the equitable dilemma students face in public-school classrooms: not feeling valued and ill-equipped to effectively dissent. This is particularly true for lower-performing students and those whom teachers view through biases, prejudices, and stereotypes inherited from social conditioning. It is Biggie's rise and commercial success from "negative to positive" that allowed him to give expression to the general thoughts and feelings of students who rarely are heard (Fontaine, 2010).

I hear them.

As an educator and school dean for 17 years in five New York City high-poverty schools—those in which more than 75 percent of the students are eligible for free or reduced-price lunch—I've heard the brokenness of students who say teachers act as if they don't see them and focus on favorites, to whom they teach more. They bemoan teachers who limit their success by setting cut-off dates to make up missed assignments. For talking out of turn to a classmate, students get their names put on a board with negative points, perhaps to "embarrass" them into compliance. A Black girl tells me, "These teachers constantly be telling me, 'you have a bad attitude,'" when what really happened is the Black girl questioned something the teacher had said or said something the teacher didn't want to hear. Black and Latino boys tell me they feel "picked on," like the teacher is poking the bear: "Trying to get me to do or say something out-of-pocket, so they have reason to kick me out of class." Black boys, particularly, say their teachers "always be warning us to stop hanging with the wrong crowd," telling them things like, "You're better than them," and "They're trouble." Those boys, in turn, ask me, "Can the teachers teach the ones they think are trouble the same way they teach the ones they favor?"

What seems to hurt students most, though, is when teachers mock or talk down to them "like we're stupid." Students across grade levels recognize what they call *subs* (subliminal language) almost as well as they read social cues. But recognizing the subliminal doesn't mean they know how to process it. They also don't know how to process teacher rhetoric shrouded, perhaps, in scare tactics or reverse psychology: "You're failing my class, so there's no need to come." For a teacher to benignly suggest psychosocially developing students quit because they're "failing" is treacherous; for the student, it can become a self-fulfilling prophecy.

Seeing Inequity

Gloria Ladson-Billings, widely recognized as the founding expert in the field of culturally relevant pedagogy, identifies two types of students deriving from historic social conditions: school-dependent and school-independent (Bassoff, 2005). Ladson-Billings posits that "school-independent students go to school, but because of the support and resources available to them at home, they could get by without formal schooling. Their parents or guardians give them opportunities that allow for experiences not otherwise offered through formal schooling." The lives of school-independent students are not without adversity or inequity, but practical systems are in place—tutors, coaches, therapy—to help them thrive.

Formal education for the school-dependent student should expand on informal learning, while also teaching academic foundations, so students lead their learning and reach their fullest social, emotional, and academic potential.

For the most part, school-dependent students, more often described as students of color, survive. Ladson-Billings says, "School-dependent children are students who need school, with all of its resources, to learn." To be clear, a great deal of informal learning for all students, culturally and otherwise, takes place outside of school—something teachers should honor. Formal education for the school-dependent student, then, should expand on informal learning, while also teaching academic foundations, so students lead their learning and reach their fullest academic, social, and emotional potential.

Create a classroom in which every student feels welcome, seen, and heard.

Here's the rub: Inequity confines school-dependent students and their families to a one-dimensional status—that of the poor. Prejudice sees those living in poverty as bereft of all things. It ignores a fact that paupers also are poets; if given equitable training and opportunity, the "poor student" can become wildly successful and inspiring; and a financially striving solo female parent cares about and invests in her child's education to the best of her capabilities. A reality is that some of the parents of school-dependent children also were school-dependent students themselves. The highest level of educational attainment for many students from Black families living in poverty is a high school diploma or GED (Hussar et al., 2020). Many fall short of that. Nonetheless, these parents see hope in education. They trust and rely heavily on educators to instruct their children nobly.

Everyone Has a Dream

What the student a teacher "favors" and the student a teacher views through a negative lens (e.g., doesn't do any work, talks too much, can't sit still, doesn't know how to behave) have in common is they both have dreams of becoming something special to the world. Students, from toddler to teen, represent the hopes and dreams of their families and caregivers. Educators are responsible for helping students deliver their dreams to their loved ones. Students see the outcomes of teachers' profound work in their mothers, fathers, and caretakers, as well as those who become world leaders, judges, doctors, musicians, athletes, librarians, dancers, designers, social-media mavens, and so on. Thus, students walk into a classroom hoping their teachers will propel them to greatness in that same magical way. Indeed, as one student told me, "Teachers are the world's biggest influencers."

Unfortunately, too many historically marginalized students—especially Black, Latine, Pacific Islander, Indigenous, and neurodiverse (those labeled with disabilities)—also know teachers can hurt them due to personal biases and assumptions. Researchers Gershenson and Papageorge analyzed the federal Education Longitudinal Study of 2002, which followed approximately 6,000 students who were in 10th grade in 2002 through 2012. The study also included surveys that asked teachers to predict how far in school each student is likely to go. The researchers found that students whose teachers had higher expectations for them are more likely to complete four years of college. Furthermore, they found that White teachers, who make up the vast majority of American educators, have far lower expectations for Black students than they do for similarly situated White students. "This evidence suggests that to raise student attainment, particularly among students of color, elevating teacher expectations, eliminating racial bias, and hiring a more diverse teaching force are worthy goals" (Gershenson & Papageorge, 2018).

Learning Phases

Critical learning phases begin early. In his landmark theory of psychosocial development, Erik Erikson says young children, ages 1 to 3, grapple with autonomy ("Can I do things on my own?"). They want to touch and explore. If the environment is overly controlling with a teacher or parent repeatedly telling them to "sit down," / "sit still," / "don't touch anything," children become rigid, ashamed, self-restricting, and non-exploratory. However, if the adults in their lives encourage agency, children develop strong will (McLeod, 2018).

Preschool children, ages 3 to 5, want to know, "Am I good or bad?" At this developmental stage, children ask questions and make fast decisions. If their efforts are met with success, they develop a sense of purpose. But if a teacher repeatedly scolds them for asking "too many" questions or exerting their newfound will, children educationally withdraw. They feel guilty for taking the initiative, so they prematurely temper this behavior.

Elementary to middle-school students, ages 6 to 12, increasingly look to their peers as they discover their place in the world. In light of newly introduced social and academic demands, they seek to gain competency. When peer competition (e.g., who gets the best grade) dominates learning, it fuels an environment in which success and self-esteem are fleeting. Those who feel they cannot compete academically may develop feelings of inferiority, while those whom teachers deem "best" embrace competence.

High school students, ages 12 to 18, reexamine who they are as they start to picture their futures as adults. Those who are comfortable with their personal and cultural identities can develop a sense of fidelity and accept others who are different from them. However, when teachers negate a student's cultural identity, they cut the student's connections to his or her native communities. When teachers don't uphold students' sexual identities, students suppress emotions. When teachers steer students away from their dreams, students flounder.

At each successive grade level, when the psychosocial needs of the school-dependent as well as the school-independent students are not taken into account and when equitable psychosocial teaching and learning are not deliberately applied, students can fall behind developmentally and academically. Elementary school teachers find themselves restoring a student's will, while also teaching purpose. Middle school teachers must sometimes restore will and purpose. By the time students reach high school, both low- and high-poverty students demonstrate a clear lack of will, purpose, and/or competency. Told too many times to sit still and be quiet, they're filled with doubt—stripped of their agency. Students who feel guilty for disrupting learning with a "stupid question" no longer raise their hands—stripped of their voice. Unsettling peer competition, such as who finishes first, makes the average and last-to-finish student feel worthless. These types of institutionalized teacher practices disrupt student learning and engagement. Feeling put off, students succumb to distraction. Ironically, students fear failure but are too psychosocially wounded and vulnerable to ask for help. They get lost in the system. Ultimately, it is the underdevelopment of students' psychosocial needs that spurs a psychosocial achievement gap—the disbelief in one's ability to succeed at a high level.

Strangleholds

In professional development workshops across several states, I've met teachers from varying grade levels who hold steadfast a belief that "underperformance" of students in high-poverty schools is the result of student noncompliance or inaction. Their quick-fix mantra: "Students just need to pay attention and focus." This oversimplified statement makes clear not all teachers recognize or understand the preoccupations of the students they instruct or what they need for both the teacher and the students to succeed.

Students have competing priorities at school and at home, in addition to their interests and dreams. Many students in high-poverty schools, for example, may worry about how to help their solo female parent pay a bill, somehow. Pressing on others' minds might be educational anxiety and a genuine, unclear understanding of how to proceed with the lesson; they don't know what questions to ask. Some also say they're bored with rote lessons that don't pique their intellectual curiosity. Indeed, within the New York City curriculum, first-through fourth-grade math students find the missing number: _?_ + 3 = 6. In seventh grade, they solve equations: $x + 3 = 6$. In ninth grade, they again find $x + 3 = 6$, only this time it's called algebra.

Many teachers I've encountered also believe if one student can learn a topic in a single lesson, others should be able to do so. These educators overlook a salient part of America's racial history. Educational policymakers and school administrators perennially shut out gifted students of color from attending "elite" public schools. So, we find unclassified gifted Black and Brown students spread throughout K–12 public-school classrooms. They sit among average and academically struggling students. Because of these cognitively accelerated students' thirst for knowledge, they may: a) act out due to monotony ["they ace the work but don't know how to behave"]; or b) do whatever a teacher tells them the minute they get the often below grade–level instruction. Teachers favor the latter because they make their job easy.

The students whom teachers identify as trouble and/or troubled—perhaps those most in need—are the ones teachers tend to ignore and/or refuse to teach. At the five New York City comprehensive schools where I've worked, administrators have liberally removed students from teachers' classrooms because the teachers have reported that the students "scared them," were "causing trouble," or were "too much to handle." K–6 teachers began referring students as young as 6 years old (first grade) to special education. Most of these are Black boys, who are classified under a banner of emotional disturbance, followed by learning disabled.

Call to Action

Students at every grade level clamor to learn. The fact that they show up for school should tell us this. It demonstrates their willingness to climb. Engaging students equitably in a classroom does not have to be a tightrope walk. It doesn't require a teacher to know every aspect of a student's background. Some of it is not a teacher's business to know. Concretely, educators must:

1) meet students where they are psychosocially and with full consideration of their social circumstances as they arrive at their classroom doors;

2) allow students access to their human capacity–building superpower by sharing their attention and knowledge perspectives; and

3) rigorously engage students with the benefit of the doubt and help them map their dreams to reality.

Moving Forward: Equitable Considerations

Below are a few abbreviated but important definitions.

Equity: the quality of being fair and impartial

Inequity: a presumptuous and unjust practice

School-dependent student: a student who needs the enriching environment of school, with all of its resources, to learn how to navigate through inequity and the demands of society

School-independent student: a student who, because of the support and resources available at home, could get by without formal schooling but still warrants appropriate psychosocial development

Psychosocial development: conscious growth and differentiation from infancy to maturity

What students need—no matter their background—is unbiased judgment, less blame, more prompting, more patience, and increased perspective from the educators in charge. During their learning transformation, indeed, the emotional unwinding of a student (or two or three!) will get on a teacher's nerves. Additionally, educators are dealing with their own set(s) of traumas, and students can trigger or be reminders of them. But maybe, just maybe, through an act of humility and reflection, students and teachers can help one another. In a moment of dissent, a challenging student should make an educator pause to ask: *Have I created a safe environment or an intolerant one? One that focuses on competitiveness and punitive compliance or one that promotes a student's psychosocial development?*

As dean, I've always told teachers, "Your worst student is your biggest challenge and the biggest test of your ability to do your job well. Don't run from that student. Don't push him or her out. Find out what makes that student tick. Use your superhero talent to vigorously develop that student. Find things other people wouldn't think of finding. Reaching that student will be your greatest reward."

Only when educators open their eyes to inequity will they see it. It's not in the hues and voices of underserved, school-dependent or school-independent students, but in an educator's actions. Inequity sits in educational policies and practices and sometimes in a teacher's thoughts and perceptions. School principals and administrators, as well as teachers, have autonomy in areas of discipline and curriculum, bathroom use, and attendance to revitalize policy so that it is not partial and diminishing for their demographic community. As service providers, educators owe students a safe space to grow, which includes providing them with:

> **Inequity sits in educational policies and practices and sometimes in a teacher's thoughts and perceptions.**

1) the time and energy to understand where they're coming from; and

2) opportunities to respectfully speak their mind and share their points of view without worrying they'll be disciplined for speaking their truths.

Recall that feel-good teacher-appreciation activity at the beginning of this essay. Each of us wants to feel valued, including all of the students whom teachers kick out of their classrooms. More than being "nice," equity warrants teachers who are instructionally deliberate with a strong sense of self, principles, and willingness to grow.

With this evolved understanding and renewed vision of what educators must *see* to achieve equity in the classroom, carefully and wisely make sure each student has a platform to be splendid, spectacular, and joyous, and to thrive! All students deserve to know what those things feel like in their educational experience and journey to independence.

Care-tactics & Humble Reminders Toward Equity

Below are some tips and ideas from my upcoming book, *26 Care-tactics & Humble Reminders Toward Equity for 26 Weeks of School*.

- An enormous educational challenge teachers face is their assumptions about students. Bias or prejudice (e.g., toward hijabs, do-rags, sagging pants, LGBTQ+ affiliations, goth appearances, ideas surrounding "proper" English, gender-specific beauty, and class) impacts how teachers regard students. Teachers must think less about student expression and focus on the lesson a student needs to soar past bigotry.

- Close your eyes and try to imagine the point of view of a student under your care. Ask yourself this question: "As this student, what would I want?" Then follow up with this question: "As this student, what would I fear?" Consider your answers. Helping the student to disable fear begins the breakthrough. It clears the pathway for learning.

- EOP (Equity on Purpose). Purposely create a classroom in which you mark absent feelings of insecurity, inadequacy, and lack of opportunity. Substitute these with abundance. On purpose, create a classroom in which every individual feels welcome, seen, and heard, and can be productive toward his or her developmental goals. Purposefully create a safe space that makes equity a protective factor for all students.

- Take a full glance at your students and acknowledge their differences. Make only one assumption: Each one needs you—your knowledge and full support—to advance to the next level. In a dignified way, teach students everything you know, especially how to succeed, one goal at a time. You, after all, are their firm example.

- The learning process is complicated. A teacher's duty is to enable students to succeed in school and in life. It starts with teachers developing will, establishing purpose, and teaching students how to set and meet goals so they competently unravel the many facets of their growing lives independently. That process begins the first day we meet them.

- I firmly believe there should be a Standard Practice Oath for Educators that all graduating teachers should take and know by heart:

  > "I, [name], promise with my full heart to nurture all students who come before me. I promise to teach them and learn from them as we grow in knowledge for the strength of humanity. I recognize I have biases, which are incomplete understandings of individuals and groups, and I promise to strive to add to my biased perspectives for the sake of human kindness and equity."

Alonzo Westbrook has spent more than 17 years working for the New York City Department of Education as a teacher, administrator, and football coach. He currently teaches high school students in Harlem. He has served as guest lecturer at various colleges and secondary schools on developmental subjects, such as resilience and culturally responsive teaching. A graduate of Morehouse College, Westbrook began his career as a journalist.

Instructional Equity: What, Why, and How

by Rachel Hsieh

"**H**ave you always taught with a social justice lens? How do you start?" These are two of the most frequently asked questions I receive along with "Where are you from?"

As a first-generation Chinese American educator who has been in the classroom for more than a decade, teaching with a social justice lens within an instructional equity framework is a skill I continually strive to improve upon. Learning is constant. Therefore, as my understanding of equity and justice teaching continues to grow, this current essay reflects what I understand now.

All teaching and learning is contextual. The majority of the staff in my school district are White presenting. In my school, I am the only identified Asian American educator of 16 classroom teachers who teach a specific grade level. I teach in a small suburban district of about 5,000 students. Across the district, our community demographics are:

- about 76 percent identify as White
- 15 percent Latine
- 2 percent Asian
- 2 percent Black
- 1 percent Indigenous and 5 percent multiracial (National Center for Education Statistics, 2015–2019)

Looking at my own classroom data from 2018 to 2021, about one-third of my fourth graders are learning English as another language, and between one fourth and two thirds identify as Black, Indigenous, or people of color.

Regardless of classroom or school demographics, teaching with an instructional equity framework is integral in any context. This is because all students deserve to be seen and listened to. Students need to know that they matter and belong. Teaching with an instructional equity framework gives students a broader view of current events and news and allows them to see themselves mirrored throughout all their learning. Teaching with an instructional equity framework involves a little extra work; however, it is worth it.

As an educator, I hope that my students are able to enter the classroom expressing their whole selves. I also hope that other educators can take the examples I share on the following pages as models to reflect on their own lessons and begin to incorporate instructional equity into their practice.

What Is Instructional Equity?

When I think about equity, one of the first words that come to mind is *access*. **Equity is about ensuring students have access to whatever they need in order to succeed.** In my fourth-grade class, one of the beginning-of-the-year activities I do with students is developing working definitions of *fair* versus *equal*. (I adapted this lesson from Katie Wich's workshop at the 2014 Northwest Teaching for Social Justice Conference.) Understanding the differences between fair and equal provides the foundation toward understanding equity.

I start by giving each student a card with a scenario written on it; for example, "I scraped my knee" or "I broke my arm." I encourage students to act out their scenarios. I intentionally start with the student with the scraped knee and give that student a bandage. After that, for every student's scenario that follows that student gets a bandage, whether or not it makes sense to. As students sit with their bandages (while others continue to act out their scenarios), there is always one who comments, "I don't need a bandage, though." I respond, "You don't? But ___ needed one for her knee, so to be fair I need to give you one for your situation." This prompts students to counter that different situations call for different things. I then ask: "As learners, do you think you all need the same thing or that you all learn the exact same way?" As students shout out "no" and try to explain, we begin to create the definitions for *fair* and *equal*. Students also begin to recognize where and how equity shows up in our classroom.

Instructional equity is a framework that guides teaching so that all members of the classroom (including teachers, educational/instructional assistants, and paraprofessionals) do their best learning. Instructional equity challenges teachers to examine the required academic content, think about their current students, reflect on their own biases, and ask whether all perspectives have been represented. Instructional equity helps build critical thinking skills. It requires relationship building and shared power. Educators teaching with an instructional equity framework do not assume they know what their students need in order to learn. Rather, they engage with students and caregivers in an ongoing conversation to learn what they need to best facilitate student learning. They allow and encourage students to initiate change and action based on their perspectives and thoughts. Instructional equity requires reflection and flexibility. It is about making content relevant to your current students and recognizing that what may have worked in previous years may not work in the current year. This recognition proves to students that they are seen and heard.

The instructional equity framework my school district developed contains five components, which I use to help ground myself when establishing a class community and planning a lesson or unit. I adapted their definitions as follows:

- **Multiple perspectives** – being able to examine and think critically about historical and current events from multiple viewpoints
- **Citizenship skills** – building skills to make informed decisions and solve problems as active citizens of the world
- **Democratic equity** – using current events to critically examine and highlight how democracy is working or not working
- **Social action** – putting knowledge to action to help change our community
- **Reflective inquiry** – taking time to critically reflect and ask questions to better understand

When I first began incorporating instructional equity, I started with only one component and slowly added more to my lessons as I became more familiar with each component. I have since added questions for my own planning. The table below lists the questions I ask myself as I plan my lessons.

Table 6. Lesson Planning Using the Instructional Equity Framework

Multiple Perspectives	Citizenship Skills	Democratic Equity	Social Action	Reflective Inquiry
• Whose story is being told in the curriculum? • Whose voice is missing? • What else could have been included in the text that could have portrayed characters differently?	• How can I guide students to form their own opinions?	• Processing current events: who, what, when, where, why? • How does what has happened affect others and myself?	• What are ways to help our local and broader community?	• What do I see? • What do I notice? • What makes me think that?

Establishing a Class Community

Prior to planning lessons and units with the instructional equity framework, it is important to establish a class community. Establishing a class community goes beyond playing fun games at the start of the year or setting up a rewards system that students need to work toward. A community represents belonging. I want all students to know and feel that they belong in our class. I want all students to know that they can have different opinions and perspectives based on individual experiences and still belong in our class community. To establish belonging means to recognize the power of relationships and the power structure within the classroom. As Cornelius Minor (2018) stated, "Creating a space where kids feel safe means that we must create a space where we share power. One can let go of power without letting go of control."

Shared power means students must have a voice in the daily happenings in the classroom. When establishing routines, norms, and expectations, we need to make sure to include students in the process rather than just relying on teacher-directed procedures that don't account for students' experiences and concerns. Letting go of power is a gradual process and can be challenging to teachers accustomed to their classrooms functioning in a certain way. However, once shared power is established, the rewards outweigh any challenges.

I often use picture books to introduce a topic for discussion, especially around fostering belonging, inclusion, and community. Some of my favorites include:

- *The Day You Begin,* by Jacqueline Woodson
- *Your Name Is a Song,* by Jamilah Thompkins-Bigelow
- *All Are Welcome,* by Alexandra Penfold
- *What Do You Do With a Problem?* by Kobi Yamada

Know Your Students

Establishing a class community requires taking time to get to know your students at an individual level, with family members, and with peers.

At the individual level this can look like individual conferences during class, quick morning check-ins at breakfast, or writing letters to students throughout the year (an activity that I adapted from the website Teaching With a Mountain View). For example, at the start of the year, I write an introductory letter to each of my students. I encourage them to write back, and I respond each time with a personalized letter answering their questions. Although not every student will write back, this activity has helped foster a deep relationship with my students and allows me a small window into their lives. The letters I've received are some of the best mementos I have from students.

Building relationships with students and their family members can mean having beginning-of-the-year conferences, sending positive messages, and sending check-ins to caregivers. For example, during the pandemic, these check-ins included asking if families needed technology assistance or access to food or other basic needs, and setting up times to meet with them. Building relationships with families also means being transparent about what is happening in the classroom. At the start of each week, I send out a short blog post highlighting the major themes, concepts, and discussion topics for the week. Families are always welcome to reach out with any questions or concerns. When they do, it is often a powerful learning opportunity for me as well. Families deserve to be heard and have a part in the shared power, too.

It is also important to take time to get to know students when they are around their peers. You can observe student interactions during free time, eat lunch with students, or join in on games during recess and PE. Getting to know my students in each of these contexts is part of helping them understand that they deserve to be seen and listened to. All students deserve a space that will welcome them as they are.

Class Meetings

Establishing a community is a continuous process. Aside from read-aloud discussions, class meetings are a crucial way to help guide the community. There are multiple types of class meetings with different purposes (Minor, 2019). Class meetings provide students space to learn and practice engaging in respectful dialogue with one another. We often start our day with fun, silly questions *(Would you rather have a pet dragon or a robot?)* and then move to deeper discussions *(What is the difference between fair and equal?)*.

Class meetings are also a critical space where students learn to identify and resolve conflicts, such as: *What is causing the class to be upset during PE games?* As a teacher, I intentionally provide students with scaffolds to facilitate dialogue and engage in meaningful and respectful conversations with one another. I model and help them use phrases such as:

- *I agree with ___ because ___.*
- *I respectfully disagree with ___ because ___.*

With repeated practice, students use these phrases in class throughout the day as they communicate and listen to one another. Class meetings provide a space for all members to recalibrate, ground, and focus themselves in the class community. Grounding ourselves in our class community allows for deeper learning, because it reminds my students that our classroom is a space where they can enter with their whole selves, bravely ask questions, and wonder.

Incorporating Instructional Equity Into Lessons and Units

When incorporating instructional equity into lessons and units, it is essential to start slow. Instead of trying to incorporate all five components into a lesson at once, first choose one to focus on and become familiar with. Instructional equity requires educators to reflect and make content relevant to their current students. The examples I share here come from recent experiences in teaching these lessons. The headings reflect the main instructional equity component I was focusing on; however, other components are also present. Note: What I refer to as *lessons* are not single, 30- to 45-minute class periods; rather, a lesson can take up to five class periods. A unit is at least four weeks long, with multiple lessons that are often integrated with multiple subjects. Incorporating instructional equity into lessons and units cannot start until a strong class community has been established.

Democratic Equity in Literacy

Identity is a year-long theme in my classroom. In building a class community where all students know that they belong and can enter with their whole selves, we spend the beginning of the year understanding ourselves and what we bring to our community. Identity is continuous work. A great place to start is to explore the Identity domain of the Social Justice Standards from Learning for Justice (learningforjustice.org).

Names are a big part of a person's identity. Names hold meaning, and they contain stories and family history. Therefore, it is essential to pronounce and spell names correctly. It is also important to ask students what they prefer to be called. This may not be a question that students are accustomed to, so they may not recognize the power they hold here. Students have often said to me, "It's okay if you call me by this name" or "It doesn't matter to me." My job as an educator is to guide students toward recognizing shared power, so here are a few ways I respond:

- *This is your name, and your name is important. I want to make sure our class gets it correct.*
- *Can you tell me what name you are most comfortable with us using?*
- *Can you say your name again so I (we) can practice?*

I also model with my name, Ms. Hsieh. I introduce myself and explain the significance of my last name, Hsieh 謝 (xiè), which means "thank you" in Chinese. It takes practice for students, families, and colleagues to get the intonations correct. However, this modeling has prompted students to advocate for themselves and correct peers on how to say their own names.

Picture books also provide a way to help students recognize the importance of names. We read *The Name Jar,* by Yangsook Choi, and *Alma and How She Got Her Name,* by Juana Martinez-Neal, and make connections with them.

In October 2020, current events provided an opportunity to reinforce the importance of names. I adapted a headline from CNN to present to my students: "Sen. David Perdue Mispronounces Sen. Kamala Harris's Name." (Note: The objective of this discussion was not politics. I wanted my students to focus more on the incident than on the presidential campaigns that were happening around that time.) In addition to the headline, I picked up this quote from the article: ". . . Kah-ma-la, or Ka-MAL-a, or Kamala, Kamala-mala-mala, I don't know, whatever" (Judd & Nobles, 2020). Then I asked my students:

- *What are your first thoughts?*
- *What do you wonder?*
- *What do you think?*
- *What do you want to say?*

Names are a big part of a person's identity. Names hold meaning, and they contain stories and family history. Therefore, it is essential to pronounce and spell names correctly.

Students commented: "He didn't ask?" "That doesn't seem nice." Most agreed Senator Perdue should have asked Senator Harris how to pronounce her name. Then, I gave my class additional information. At the time, Senators Harris and Perdue were working together on a committee. Students were outraged. I added a wondering out loud for my students to think about: "Perhaps Senator Perdue doesn't think Senator Harris's name is a normal name so had a hard time saying it. What do you think? Who gets to decide if a name is normal?" Students argued back, stating that the senator was being disrespectful and what does *normal* mean anyway. One student asserted, "All names are beautiful, and there is no such thing as a normal name. Names are from [a person's] cultures, their lives, and they're all beautiful."

Students were able to take a current event, process it, and relate it to their own lives. As we wrapped up this discussion, the final consensus was that this was a disrespectful event, and perhaps in the future Senator Perdue could just ask before making such a comment, especially as a public figure. (Note: As stated earlier, the objective of this discussion was not politics. If a student had brought up politics, I would have redirected by saying, "Let's refocus on this event at this moment.")

The instructional equity framework also gives students chances to revisit, reengage, and deepen their understanding and literacy around what we have been learning. We revisited the names discussion when we read the book *Your Name Is a Song*. Again, students affirmed that the correct way to pronounce a name is determined by the individual, not by others. As another student stated, "Every name is unique because every name has its own reason."

Multiple Perspectives in Social Studies

Fourth-grade social studies in Oregon centers around Oregon history, particularly the Lewis and Clark expedition and the Oregon Trail. While these are important events in history, the adopted curriculum portrays one perspective—that of Lewis and Clark as heroes and that those who traveled on the Oregon Trail arrived to claim lands that were open, uninhabited, and free.

As an educator, I believe it is important to share history from multiple perspectives. Before I begin to teach about the Lewis and Clark expedition, I first need to build up students' understanding about Indigenous people and what Oregon was like prior to the arrival of Lewis and Clark. I personally choose to start this lesson close to the second week of October to link it to a federal holiday. However, Indigenous history—or any history or heritages—should be taught year-round. This lesson is a sequence of days that look like this:

- Assess students' prior knowledge of Indigenous people
- Explore and examine the Native Land map (native-land.ca)
- Assess students' prior knowledge of Christopher Columbus
- Pose question: "Should the second Monday of October still be called Columbus Day, or should it be called Indigenous Peoples' Day?" (Note: On October 11, 2021, President Joe Biden issued a proclamation recognizing Indigenous Peoples' Day at the federal level. However, many calendars still note the day as Columbus Day.)

Again, an established class community must be in place before this lesson can begin. There are students in my class who identify as Indigenous. Prior to this lesson, I had talked to them to help prepare them for their peers' responses. How a person identifies and decides to share is a personal choice. In past years, some students have chosen to share their backgrounds earlier in the school year when we first discuss identities, while others choose to share during this lesson or after. In addition, I have alerted families of the lesson in my weekly blog post and invited them to discuss any concerns with me. There is no expectation that my Indigenous students need to share or speak up during the lesson unless they would like to. This again relates to class community and what students are comfortable with.

I begin the lesson by asking students, "What comes to mind when you hear the words *Native American* or *Indigenous*?" Students draw and jot down words that come to mind. Most often students' drawings include people in braids with feathers, trees, animals, huts, and tipis. After all students have had a chance to share their drawings and words, I ask, "Why might some people think Indigenous people exist only in the past?"

After a quick survey of responses, I introduce students to contemporary Indigenous people—authors of books we have read in class, athletes, members of Congress, artists, student activists—and show pictures of them. Students reflect using the language pattern, "I used to think ___, but now I know/think ___." A common response from students is, "I now know that Indigenous people are just like us."

Once students have established the understanding that Indigenous people are here today, I introduce the Native Lands map, asking:

- *What do you see?*
- *What do you wonder?*
- *What do you think?*
- *Whose land are we on?*

[Native Americans]
1st / Initial thoughts:

- olden times
- wear hats or headresses w/ feathers
- travel by boat
- cut down trees to make homes or tools
- hunt animals for food
- string to make bows
- wearing leaves, feathers
- fighting, war
- singers
- rocks to make arrows

AFTER seeing pictures:
- just like other Americans
- have different skin colors
- as good as we are / nice
- look better in real life than in OR Trail game
- wear clothes similar to ours
- no longer engage in wars
- can do whatever they want
- do the same things 'we do
- do not always have the same rights - are treated differently

I used to think_____ (only) _____ but now I know_____

At first I thought _____ Now I think_____

After their initial observations, we discuss whose land our school is on, and students explore whose land their homes and other places are on. We also begin to map places in Oregon as another part of this lesson.

As I mentioned earlier, I personally make time to teach this lesson early in October to have students form their opinions on whether the second Monday in October should still be called Columbus Day. While the day is now federally recognized as Indigenous Peoples' Day, many commercials and ads still advertise Columbus Day as a big sale day. To open the discussion, I ask students if they have heard of Christopher Columbus. In the last few years I've noticed that students recognize the name from seeing it on a calendar more than what Columbus is "known" for. So I follow up with this query: "I wonder what he has done to have a whole day dedicated to him?" I introduce *Encounter* by Jane Yolen. (Note: *Encounter* is not a perfect book. It includes an author's note that is problematic. Therefore, based on feedback from a mentor, I am currently looking for another book to use.) We start with a picture walk so students have a chance to make predictions and engage with the story through images first. When I begin the story, I ask students to pay attention to who is telling the story, from whose perspective this story is being told, and how that affects the events in the story, and also to notice the exchange between the two groups of people.

Once we have finished reading the book, I ask my students about their impressions of Christopher Columbus and whether there should still be a day dedicated to him. There is always a mix of very passionate noes along with some unsure responses. We then read articles from *Newsela* and *Scholastic News* and invite local Indigenous scholars to speak with the class.

After spending time learning and gathering information, we come together to write a response to this question: "Should the second Monday of October still be called Columbus Day, or should it be called Indigenous Peoples' Day?" Students cite reasons and discuss both sides before I ask them to write independently, using these language patterns:

- *The second Monday of October should be called ___ because ___.*
- *We should/should not celebrate ___ because ___.*

Students are allowed to have different perspectives, of course. If students are able to make a strong argument for what the second Monday of October should be known for, then the lesson's objectives were met. We can then take this knowledge into our study of Lewis and Clark's expedition and use a critical lens to think about the impacts of their journey.

Here are additional books I read with my class and have in my classroom.

- *The People Shall Continue,* by Simon J. Ortiz
- *We Are Still Here!* by Traci Sorell
- *Go Show the World: A Celebration of Indigenous Heroes,* by Wab Kinew
- *Fry Bread, A Native American Family Story,* by Kevin Noble Maillard

Citizenship, Social Action, and Reflective Inquiry in Math

Instructional equity is also critically important in mathematics. Mathematics is often assumed to have a single answer and single strategy to obtain the answer. However, mathematics can be full of lively discourse if students are given the opportunity to solve problems using the strategies that they are most comfortable with or have learned from others aside from the textbook. Applying instructional equity in mathematics means allowing for multiple perspectives and a flexibility for students to showcase their math knowledge beyond the standard algorithms and formulas.

Multiplication is a major math standard to cover in fourth grade. Rather than teaching formulas and algorithms for students to memorize, I decided to incorporate a community issue that students had brought up earlier in the year and create a project in which students use multiplication and measurement to build model tiny houses. In our community, tiny houses are being used as transitional housing for people experiencing homelessness. (Note: Since teaching this unit, I have changed my wording from *homeless* to *houseless* or *unhoused*.)

There are students in my class who are navigating various living situations. Prior to starting this unit, I reached out and talked to them and asked about their comfort level. They have the power to let me know when the project becomes too overwhelming and they need to take a break or stop. This is not a unit I would have continued if I was not confident that we had built a strong class community.

The topic of homelessness began as a discussion in our class about what is a human right and what are examples of rights that every human should have. Students stated that every human should have the right to a place to live and that this was an issue within our own community. I asked if there was a way we could help. In this particular year, we had also just voted for Oregon's Kid Governor. (This is a statewide program for fifth graders to experience the election process. My class participated as active voters and learned about voting rights in the United States, past and present.) There were a few candidates, but most students chose the candidate who ran with the platform to help people navigating homelessness. Our initial class discussions centered around these essential questions:

- What does it mean to be homeless?
- How can we help those who are navigating homelessness?

Students had additional questions, which I used to help build the unit to reflect their inquiries and work toward social action and citizenship.

- Why or how do people become homeless?
- Why can't homeless people get a job?
- Why are their clothes all ripped up?
- Why can't homeless people just go to the shelter?
- What do they need?

Based on my class's questions, I could see we needed to do some reading and discussion around homelessness and unhoused people. There were also some biases and stereotypes to overcome. As their teacher, I provide facts for students to form their own opinion and recognize their own biases and stereotypes.

We spent a couple days reading and understanding national and local data. Integrating math skills into this activity, students wrote comparison statements based on the data presented on the graphs. For example, 129,927 (California's homeless population in 2018) > 14,478 (Oregon's homeless population in 2018). Students did a gallery walk, writing and discussing what they saw on the various graphs. Examining the data helped prove our claims that this was a significant issue within our community. It also helped reinforce students' responsibility as citizens of our community: *Was this an issue that they thought is important enough to try to help solve?* All agreed that this issue was important, especially after noticing that our state ranked fifth in the nation, and we began to build our tiny house models.

My students—the primary architects and designers—followed this design process:

- Calculate the areas and perimeters of different floor plans.
- Decide who their house would be designed for: one person, two people, three or more people, with or without pets.
- Determine what essential furniture and appliances are needed versus what are considered extras.
- Draft an initial house blueprint, taking note of area and perimeter of all spaces (including doors and windows), furniture, and appliances.
- Purchase essential furniture and appliances, while also calculating costs so as not to exceed their given budget.
- Edit and revise the initial house blueprint to match the purchased essentials list, and recalculate areas and perimeters.
- Complete a final draft of the house blueprint and construct a paper model of their tiny house.

Throughout this entire process, I acted as a facilitator, notetaker, and questioner for my students. When students were deciding who their house would be for, I guided them through a discussion about who do we most often see navigating homelessness in our community and whether who we see represents everyone. As students purchased and decided on essential items, they compared lists and worked together as a class to determine what are the top essential items and what are extra. While they placed their furniture in the houses, I asked about their placement choices and room designs. Were they keeping the recipients of the house in mind throughout the entire process? By acting in these roles, I supported my students in building their citizenship skills, social action, and reflective inquiry. Students needed to defend their purchases and explain their furniture placement and design choices. They also had to be open to critique and wonderings from peers about their houses.

Toward the end of this unit, students began to ask how their houses could be seen beyond our local community. So, we issued two invitations: one to the state senator representing our district and one to the newly appointed Kid Governor. Both visited my class and talked to my students about homelessness.

While there is much that still needs to be done to combat this community issue, my students came out of this experience feeling heard and listened to. In fact, the Kid Governor held a fundraiser later in the year and donated some of the money raised to our school. Students had a stronger and more empathetic understanding of people navigating homelessness. Students were able to use their power to make some change in elected officials. Then, as we processed current events in spring 2020—learning how to stay safe in the pandemic, hearing about and seeing racial justice protests—students were able to use their power to listen to one another and hear one another's perspectives.

Summary

At its core, instructional equity is about making content relevant to your current students. It is a framework that can be layered in with state standards and social justice standards. What I have provided here are examples from my current teaching. It is not perfect. Instructional equity is challenging to implement without first establishing a strong class community that welcomes students and families as they are. My entry point for integrating instructional equity into my teaching was to bring in counternarratives and multiple perspectives to balance the district-adopted curriculum, and it gradually grew from there. Incorporating instructional equity is a gradual process. Expect mistakes. Expect questions. Be flexible and transparent. Recognize that lessons or activities that may have worked in previous classes may not work in current classes.

Which lesson will you reflect on and revise to incorporate one instructional equity component? Critical and reflective teaching requires taking risks. What risks are you willing to take as an educator for students to know that they belong?

Rachel Hsieh is a teacher and coach currently based in Oregon. She believes strongly in centering student voice in the classroom and learning alongside her students. She continues to grow in her understanding of becoming an anti-bias, anti-racist educator.

Spotlight on Third-Grade Literacy Proficiency for Black and Brown Youth

by Maria Armstrong, Ed.D.

I come from a family that is Latino of *mestizo* (mixed Spanish and Indigenous) background and has lived in the United States for over nine generations. My mother had me at the age of 16 with a ninth-grade education. My father, who was 10 years her senior, had received his GED at the age of 18 when he entered the U.S. Army. My mom considered him the one with the greater understanding of all things. Yet in my earliest memories of learning, my mom was the one who sat with me night after night, helping me learn to read the words in my Dick and Jane books. My mom did not read *to* me, however. She left that to my dad, who read to me "the greatest story ever told." The stories of the Bible have always fascinated me. The way my dad read the stories created a visual understanding for me. These are my earliest memories of learning to read—until my formal education began when I entered kindergarten.

I recall my first day of kindergarten. I was not like some of the children who wouldn't let go of their parents' hands and cried at the thought of being separated. I walked right into the classroom with my waist-long hair divided into two neat braids. Shortly after all the adults had vanished, the teacher called out my name along with some other children, and we were escorted into a different classroom. I stayed in that classroom throughout the rest of the day. What I found out later was that I had been placed into an English-language learner (ELL) classroom—because on my enrollment form, my mom had checked a box indicating we spoke Spanish at home, even though English was our primary language. By the time my mom picked me up from school, I must have stored up a whole day's worth of tears because the minute I saw her they flowed freely down my cheeks. She walked me into the main office, demanding to speak with whomever was in charge and refusing to leave until her daughter was placed "in the right class."

My parents understood the importance of education, especially of reading. Research shows that children in kindergarten and first grade who have difficulties with critical phonological skills—knowledge of letter names, phonemic awareness, ability to match sound to print, and so on—are likely to be poor readers in fourth grade (Torgesen, 2004). Students who still struggle with decoding words by fourth grade will have difficulty comprehending the more complex texts they have to read in various subject areas, making it hard for them to succeed in school. Furthermore, poor reading skills have also been linked to social, emotional, and behavioral health issues (Morgan et al., 2012).

So it doesn't bode well for our children when results from the 2019 National Assessment of Education Progress, a nationwide standardized test given every two years, show that about two thirds of all fourth graders read below proficient level. When broken down by racial background, 77 percent of Brown fourth graders and 82 percent of Black fourth graders scored below proficient reading levels (Kids Count Data Center, 2022). What is happening here?

A student's familiarity with words is dependent on her upbringing or background knowledge.

The Road to Literacy

Throughout my 30-plus years of experience as both a parent and an educator, I have raised others' eyebrows when I share that teaching children is one of our society's greatest experiments. Case in point is the ongoing "war" on the best way to teach reading, based on individual or visceral interpretation. The debate about whole language, phonics, and a balanced approach to literacy is alive and strong. With five generations of educators in a school district, there are bound to be differing opinions about each of these methodologies. But what will result in the most equitable approach? Let's start by looking at what the research says.

Decoding Words

Since the 1820s, researchers have offered various methods and strategies for teaching reading. The common denominators in much of the research have been phonics, memory, and auditory functions. In 1967, Ken Goodman defined the "three-cueing strategy," which prompts children to look at picture clues, sentence syntax, and letters or word parts to identify words. This strategy is the basis of the whole language approach and balanced literacy, which have been widely used to teach children how to read. When a student comes across a word that he or she cannot read, a typical strategy is to look at the picture and guess the word. One problem with this approach is that it turns the child's attention away from the word and toward the picture. What happens down the road when the books the child reads no longer have pictures?

Decades of cognitive science research have shown that the three-cueing strategy is flawed. The "science of reading" emphasizes the importance of phonics in teaching children to read. Children need to learn how to connect

Check for Auditory Issues

Some children have difficulty distinguishing sounds—an important skill in learning phonics. Repeated ear infections have been linked to developed auditory processing issues. Parents or caregivers of a child who has a history of ear infections need to communicate this to the child's teacher early in the school year, so the teacher can think of and apply strategies for accommodation.

One such accommodation is a mini-microphone, which teachers and students can wear around the neck with a lanyard. When a teacher speaks in front of or behind the class, some students have difficulty hearing, let alone understanding, what the teacher says. Mini-microphones allow teachers and students not only to hear themselves speaking but also to hear the enunciation of every word. Teachers and students who use mini-microphones shared that the device is as valuable as any tablet, pen, or book for the benefit of sounding out words, pronunciation, and enunciation.

sounds with letters so they can use this knowledge to decode words. For example, if a child learns the sound of 10 letters, the child can read:

- 350 three-sound words (e.g., *bed*, *sad*, *pan*)
- 4,320 four-sound words (e.g., *sled*, *dress*)
- 21,650 five-sound words (e.g., *brand*, *spend*)

(Ordetx, 2021)

My point is this: Teaching and learning is and should be an evolutionary process based on research, theory, and practice. We need to provide children with tools that we know work when teaching them how to read. Currently, several school districts and universities offer teachers professional learning in the science of reading. A growing number of districts across the U.S. make it mandatory for all elementary school teachers to receive training and micro-credentialing in the science of reading. These bold initiatives speak loudly to their commitment to ensuring third-grade literacy proficiency.

When children know how to decode words (how to read the words they can say), then they're on their way to understanding what they read. But there's more to reading comprehension than simply decoding. Another important component we need to address is language comprehension. Research shows that reading comprehension is a product of children's decoding skills and their language comprehension, or ability to understand spoken language (Gough & Tunmer, 1986).

Comprehending the Spoken Language

Language comprehension includes knowing not only words and their definitions, but also how language works (e.g., grammar and syntax). As a former high school principal, I faced many students who struggled in reading and, therefore, struggled in writing. Many spoke English and Spanish but were fluent in neither language, much like I was. This made me acutely aware of how to identify the difference between multilingual learners and students who still need to learn how to read. I would often engage students in conversation about their interests and their dominant language at home. Many of them were third- and fourth-generation Americans, yet they struggled with language and literacy.

When you come from a home where you speak English, but your parents or grandparents often speak only Spanish, there are a host of dynamics in the development of language. On the one hand, you are bilingual but not biliterate. On the other hand, you may be considered a multilingual learner—like I was in kindergarten—and placed in inappropriate courses that exacerbate the issue. This misunderstanding of language and learning is a huge problem in our schools.

The formality of speech is also important, particularly for Black and Brown children. We have generations of Black and Brown communities where English slang is embedded. I, for one, use Spanglish, slang, and formal English. Research shows that "children whose home and school dialects differ are at a greater risk for reading difficulties because tasks such as learning to decode are more complex for them" (Brown et al., 2015). Julie Washington, one of the researchers and a speech pathologist at Georgia State University, says that schools need to understand that children who are heavy dialect users may need more time and more help to be successful at reading (Hanford, 2020). Respecting our differences and the fact that we all move in and out of various situations, we must teach our students when it is appropriate to use which type of speech, based on environment and setting. Being able to navigate and communicate in diverse settings will help our students grow within our communities with a respect for who they are and where they come from.

Building Background Knowledge and Vocabulary

Focusing on fundamental skills is only one part of the big picture when bridging the gap for third-grade literacy. Teaching reading is not simply a science and an art—it must also be contextual and familiar. A child's familiarity or experience with words is dependent on his or her upbringing or background knowledge.

Background knowledge is a powerful tool for mitigating gaps in learning. Growing up in a *barrio*, I did not see anything remotely aligned to what I was reading or watching on television. Many of the challenges in communities of color stem from generational poverty and lack of opportunity. A middle-class family, for example, can afford to travel for vacations, visit museums, or send their child to summer enrichment camps. All of these experiences expose the child to a lot of content and knowledge-building opportunities. A child from a low-income family, on the other hand, is less likely to have such opportunities to build background knowledge.

A child's familiarity or experience with words is dependent on his or her upbringing or background knowledge.

Vocabulary may also be limited in families of low socioeconomic standing. I found this in my own experience as a young mother, who quite frankly did not have time to think about reading different books to expand my child's vocabulary. I read the same storybooks repeatedly, so my child heard the same words again and again. When I myself was a little girl reading with my mom, I remember that we used context clues to figure out the story I was reading, but the understanding or definition of a word was all too often missing. We would simply rush on to the next word or sentence. I later learned from my father that the dictionary was an important resource for understanding what words mean—a strategy that would seem intuitive to most families today. I know that feeling of frustration that comes from not being able to understand or relate to the text.

How do we build vocabulary and provide background knowledge for students with diverse backgrounds and upbringing? We read them stories they can relate to. We provide materials that are relevant to their various experiences. I am not a revisionist by any stretch, but I think about how as an adult I am drawn to the works of Isabel Allende or Clarissa Pinkola Estés. No one should have to wait until adulthood to see themselves in books. Communities can help provide print-rich environments, such as books with diverse stories and relational histories, for families with limited resources. We do this not only to validate our children, but to close the cultural learning gaps in understanding one another. This is the power of reading—becoming literate so we can engage in a vast array of cultures.

Demand Inclusive Reading and Learning Materials

As consumers, we like to make informed decisions about the things we purchase. If we find out that something unjust or unethical went into the production of certain goods, we have been known to boycott them. Why not use our purchasing power to ensure our students are seen and provided a voice in the materials they learn from?

Many companies today seek input from educators on how to improve products and services. Very early on in my career as an assistant principal, I worked with an educational publisher on a software program to assist our high school multilingual learners. The program was very rudimentary with graphics that were inferior to those in today's learning software programs. Nonetheless, we tried to provide an alternative method of delivering instruction to supplement and give attention to the individual learning needs of students. That was well over 20 years ago. Today, we have champion publishing companies that make great strides in soliciting input and publishing stories and materials that showcase people of color as protagonists. This commitment to reaching every reader by validating their culture and race has been a long time coming and must continue.

Community Responsibility

The responsibility of literacy proficiency should not fall on classroom teachers alone. The time children spend reading a book with a parent, grandparent, big sister, brother, babysitter, auntie, uncle, or friend is time spent with a "teacher." Karen Mapp, a senior lecturer at the Harvard Graduate School of Education, says educators are finally recognizing just how necessary families are as partners in an equitable education approach (Stoltzfus, 2021). Her ongoing research shows that family engagement increases rates of literacy acquisition among children and boosts academic achievement. We all take part in teaching our next generation that learning is a community responsibility and that reading is an educational right for everyone. It is our collective responsibility within our national, state, and local communities.

Teach From a Place of Strength

The concept of professional learning communities (PLCs) or communities of practice has been around for quite some time. A PLC could be, for example, a grade-level teaching team that works collaboratively to ensure that students learn. What if we adapt this concept and utilize the teacher who is best at teaching a particular concept or skill to instruct the entire group of grade-level students? For instance, let's say one teacher in the kindergarten PLC is exceptional at teaching phonemic awareness. Why not have that teacher teach phonemic awareness to the entire kindergarten group while the other kindergarten teachers facilitate the learning experience? This way, teachers within the kindergarten group don't just talk about what they need to do for individual students; they also ensure the best, first instruction, which is critical to an equitable education.

Rotating teachers through the curriculum based on their particular strengths allows for all students to have the best learning experience their teachers can provide. Not all teachers are stellar in every facet of the curriculum—and they will be the first to admit it. It is rare to find a teacher who is passionate about both literacy and numeracy. Could PLCs evolve from one of group discussion to one of group empowerment that provides best, first instruction? Yes. In fact, this is not a new idea. A district in Washington state has intentionally been practicing this for several years, and they have seen significant growth in teacher retention and students' social, emotional, and academic learning.

The concept of community responsibility is not new. Communities around the country have challenged the status quo and brought students, teachers, parents, government officials, businesses, and education leaders together to assess and address poverty, healthcare, and education. Their sole focus is to make their community centered around services to address literacy proficiency. Services, such as before- and after-school activities for pre-kindergarten to third grade, are supplemented with technology and 1:1 tutoring in fun and innovative ways. Pre-kindergarten facilities hire certified trained staff who specialize in how to teach reading. They offer reading circles, writing tables, and, most important, play. Our communities can offer safe places for pre-kindergartners to enjoy reading-time circles at the mall, after school, in church, and in other resource centers. In addition, schools can empower older students to coach young readers or offer peer-to-peer reading opportunities. These communities are committed to ensuring all children, regardless of race or socioeconomic status, are proficient at reading and writing by third grade.

> **The time has come to work on solving one of the most fundamental rights for all children: the teaching and learning of reading and prioritizing that critical benchmark of third-grade literacy.**

Our students, our schools, our greatest assets are reflected in our communities. We cannot continue to work in segregated silos and expect to evolve as a people or as a nation. Partnerships aligned with core values and principles lie in the communities we live in and love. Centered in the working relationships of problem solving, communities will take root in a flourishing system to ensure literacy is a right to be had by all. The time has come to work on solving one of the most fundamental rights of all children: the teaching and learning of reading and prioritizing that critical benchmark of third-grade literacy. As parents, caregivers, students, educators, and policy makers, we must continue to advocate for our youth and seek better ways of ensuring a world-class education. Anything short of that is not at all equitable and is just not good enough.

Maria Armstrong, Ed.D., is the executive director for the Association of Latino Administrators & Superintendents in Washington, D.C. Education was her second career. She has served as a teacher, counselor, assistant principal, and principal, before advancing through various administrative positions as a director of multilingual learners, assistant superintendent of curriculum and instruction, superintendent at Woodland Joint USD in California, and an educational consultant for the Puerto Rico Department of Education Hurricane Maria recovery efforts. Dr. Armstrong is a proud alumna of Azusa Pacific University, where she earned her master's in education with an emphasis on counseling. She is also honored to be a recipient of the university's Influence Award. Most recently, Dr. Armstrong was named one of the Top 20 Female Leaders of the Education Industry by the American Consortium for Equity in Education.

Equity and Justice in the Classroom and Beyond

by Celeste M. Bryant, MSW

"Education is the great equalizer."
—HORACE MANN

"Education is the great equalizer," an often-quoted and abbreviated version of a statement by 19th-century education pioneer Horace Mann, is frequently embraced for its surface-level meaning. The quote is often used to perpetuate the notion that Americans have equal access to education—and, given this access, if we work hard and go to school, all Americans will experience life equitably and enjoy the wealth of riches and resources that life in such an exceptional country provides. When one delves more deeply, however, and explores the breadth of Mann's philosophy, we are challenged to think more critically about the role of education as a tool that can be used for the greater good—and that also can be a purveyor and perpetrator of inequality.

The body of literature and the number of educators committed to ensuring that education fulfills its role of creating a just society is growing. This essay examines education through a critical systemic lens, the context of which trickles down into the classroom experience. It consolidates the input and hands-on experience of 50 stakeholders, the majority of whom are teachers, along with parents, mental and physical health professionals, community leaders, curriculum specialists, education policy experts, justice advocates, and faith leaders.

"Equity in education does not truly exist," says Linda A., a public-school teacher in Springdale, Maryland. "Schools are structurally inequitable at the onset." Many education advocates have pointed to the way the funding structure of the American educational system—sourced from an unequal local tax base—creates disparity in quality of education and access to resources.

The disparities do not end there. A report published in February 2019 by EdBuild documents that non-White school districts populated mostly by Black and Brown students receive a staggering $23 billion less in funding compared to majority White school districts. Moreover, the predominantly White school districts are receiving this windfall while serving significantly fewer students. Bill L., a social justice advocate and faith leader based in Washington, D.C., opines: "A budget is a moral statement, as it reflects in its allocation of resources the values of an institution, whom it values, what it values, and who is deserving of more or less. Society should ask itself why."

Lack of equity in school funding is mirrored by lack of equity in curriculum materials. The vast majority of curricula presents a skewed and non-inclusive perspective of history. The dominance of Eurocentric materials and resources is damaging to students, communities, and the greater society. "This bias is evident in literature choices and the representation of the origins and evolution of the critical science and mathematical methods—many of which can trace their history back to non-European cultures," says Sara R., a former elementary education teacher and extracurricular math specialist from Chicago, Illinois. Gay B., a sixth-grade teacher on Long Island, NY, states, "The curriculum is sending subliminal messages to students of color, women, and LGBTQ+ that they don't matter and have not contributed to the building of the nation nor the world."

> "Every day, every human is learning things in many domains. School is the one place where we should be able to wrestle with whether what we are learning is the way things really are."
>
> —CELESTE S., MD and behavioral-health professional, NY

Educators have a front-row seat to the impact of inequality in education. While teachers may not have control over the decisions of school districts, the quality and relevance of state standards, or even the dictates of the school administration, we do have latitude with how we deliver daily instruction and in the relationships we have with our students. Alison D., a parent of two, social justice advocate, and faith leader from Washington, D.C., offers this challenge to educators: "Teachers, ask yourselves—you have the power—how are you going to use it to do good?"

This essay provides a model for incremental change at the classroom level. It offers practical recommendations of potential best practices and innovative approaches aimed to move us toward establishing a more just and equitable classroom and society.

Equity-Based Instruction

As engaged citizens, educators can play a role in all areas of equity and justice, but the power to make significant change occurs in our instructional domain. Omar I., an educational policy expert and educational grant-making leader from San Mateo, California, asserts: "We should delve more deeply into recognizing the critical role of the classroom as a vessel for student social well-being and social-emotional learning and leveraging a student's cultural identity, families, community assets, identity, and sense of self-worth as an avenue to prepare students to be proactive and engaged citizens." As John B., an art teacher in Washington, D.C., public schools, states, "Equity means you have a voice in the outcome of your learning experience."

> **"Teachers should engage in self-reflection to improve daily instruction that is inclusive of achieving equity and justice in the classroom and beyond."**
>
> –MOLLIE J., sixth-grade teacher, NY

Giving students voice, making space for their identity, and teaching them to look at their communities and the larger society through an equitable lens require us as educators to interrogate our instructional practices and intentionally maintain sustainable, equity-based teaching methodologies. The 10 Self-Reflection Questions (page 99) provide a helpful framework for implementing and strengthening equitable instructional practices.

Strategies for Building Equitable Classrooms

Equity is an instructional approach rather than a singular action. Self-reflection is a continuous process that must incorporate practical instructional changes. To establish equitable classrooms, teachers must engage in this cyclical process and identify a broad range of quantifiable, measurable, high-impact strategies that promote student engagement—and assess these strategies on an ongoing basis.

10 Self-Reflection Questions

1. What am I doing differently in instruction that is an improvement from what I did last year, last week, and yesterday? What do I expect my daily, weeklong, or yearly plan to look like?

2. What is one strategy I can employ throughout all my teaching that would improve outcomes that align with equity and justice?

3. Do I have access to vetted curriculum resources? How do I incorporate this critical pedagogy and newly learned knowledge about equity and justice into the classroom in an integrated fashion and not just as an enhancement or separate task?

4. What knowledge do I want my students to gain? (a) What skills do I want them to practice and learn? (b) How will I measure progress?

5. What can I do to improve my instruction and my classroom management to benefit student learning? (a) Am I reaching everyone, and if not, why not? (b) What does this student or my class require so they can learn?

6. What ongoing support do I need and who can provide it?

7. Who are my allies in the school and with whom can I partner to collaborate to improve equity and justice in my classroom?

8. Am I practicing fairness and equity in grading, assessment, and discipline and in other evaluative tasks? Are my expectations for my students high and commensurate with their individual learning needs and capacity to engage and learn?

9. Have I planned instructional opportunities for students to have choice in their learning and give voice to their needs? Have I planned instructional opportunities to link what they are learning in the classroom with their contemporary experience? Is it reflective of opportunities to incorporate each student's culture, family, and context of the surrounding community?

10. How can I communicate learning goals with families and caregivers and offer specific actions they can take to connect learning in school to the home and the community?

The following pedagogical approaches, engagement strategies, and learning activities derive from the *realistic lens* and *practical experiences* of the 50 classroom educators and stakeholders interviewed for this essay. These practical, evidence-based techniques center the student experience, utilize relevant teaching tools, and offer opportunities for transformational learning.

> **"Teachers must learn instructional strategies that reflect how to engage students in discussions that incorporate inclusive curriculum, critical pedagogy, and self-reflection."**
>
> —CATHERINE F., sixth-grade private-school teacher, VA

Implementing Inclusive Instruction

"ALL children can learn and achieve. That is a fundamental tenet of teaching," says Thomas K., a retired principal of Philadelphia public schools. Yet, inequitable practices can be pervasive in the daily instructional practices currently being implemented in schools and classrooms. Practices such as tracking and teaching to "the test" dampen the opportunity for dynamic learning and exchange with students. Inclusive instruction reaches beyond rote instruction or limited expectations on student capability to engage learners on multiple levels with multiple approaches.

Here are some equitable approaches for reaching all learners:

- **Embrace alternative solution thinking when it comes to problem solving.** Focus on student strengths and not incorrect answers. This will lead to children feeling mastery and achievement of self-efficacy. We can encourage learners and activate the learning process by responding to right answers and "wrong" answers with prompts, such as: *How did you arrive at that conclusion? Here is what works about your process. Let's all work together to find ways to improve on that conclusion.*

- **Make math less abstract and connect it with what's happening in the world.** Use math in a unbiased way to examine trends and acknowledge differences and disparities. Allow room for disagreement about interpretations and to discuss and debate the conclusions students draw. Consult curriculum experts who are doing groundbreaking work in math to improve math education and connect to real-world experience. Experts, such as Citizen Math (citizenmath.com), MAPSCorps (mapscorps. org), and Math Circles (mathcircles.org) offer creative ways to adopt curricula that excite students about math. They are committed to helping students understand that math formulas and procedures can be applied to everyday life experiences and lead to drawing unbiased and evidence-based conclusions.

- **Engage in cross-discipline study through collaboration with other teachers, or create your own opportunities for students to study and evaluate an issue holistically.** Cross-discipline study enables students to examine a subject from different perspectives and enhances critical and creative thinking. For example, if you study the Harlem Renaissance period, integrate the music of the period during art, explore its literature during English, and examine the world economy and scientific innovations during math and science.

Building Responsive and Supportive Classroom Structure

In far too many of our schools, the disciplinary policies are structured to reflect the punitive justice system in the greater society. Inequitable methods of discipline, such as biased disciplinary measures and policing in schools, sets up pipelines to the criminal justice system for Black and Brown children at disproportionately high levels. Equitable classrooms interrupt the school-to-prison pipeline by acknowledging trauma, working with students through their developmental stages, and providing supportive opportunities for age-appropriate growth. Jazmine B., a university diversity expert and former school teaching aide from Virginia, asserts: "Facilitating restorative justice methods or enforcing logical consequences allow children to examine their behavior and negotiate reasonable consequences."

> "Problem solving is different than just learning facts. To be educated is to have the ability to critically analyze the facts and information you are being given."
>
> —CHRISTOPHER C., doctoral student in special education, MD

Encourage students to approach problems from different angles and to explain their thinking.

Here are some methods for building a responsive and supportive classroom culture:

- **Conduct "morning meetings" or "circle shares"** to check in at the beginning, middle, or end of the day to impart social-emotional learning and offer opportunities for students to voice concerns. These moments may also play a preventative role by allowing students to vent issues that might distract from learning. Consider partnering with nurses, health educators, school counselors, and social workers to facilitate these discussions.

- **Integrate social-emotional learning and general life-skills development across all subjects.** Specific instruction in social-emotional learning and purposeful probing during discussions, project-based learning, and experiential exercises can provide teachable moments and ample opportunities for students to learn and express empathy, engage in active listening, and practice patience with difference. This rich context allows critical thinking and analysis, negotiating, and conflict resolution skills to develop and flourish. Teaching students not to see threat in difference is important. Encourage students to explore questions such as: *How do you feel personally? Does this anger or frustrate you? How can you express these feelings appropriately and in a non-harmful way? How do you think other people might feel in this situation?*

  > "We must get to know the needs of a student and open ourselves up to the totality of their experience."
  >
  > —HEATHER H.,
  > Baltimore public schools

  Additionally, teaching students to acknowledge and resolve cognitive dissonance, in which they believe two opposing viewpoints, is critical. Where evidence is present that contradicts assumptions, students must learn to disengage from a belief that is contradictory. Examples of general probing questions include: *What does the evidence say about this issue? Is your belief supported by the evidence?*

- **Avoid using role plays, case studies, or other experiential exercises that are harmful to students.** Role plays, case studies, and storytelling are vital, practical, and evidence-based tools for developing critical thinking and social-emotional learning skills. However, as with all instruction, utilizing such approaches must be conducted with clear intention. In December 2021, students at an elementary school in Washington, D.C., were forced to reenact the Holocaust in class, with one child assigned to play Hitler. Such reenactments are harmful to students and many others. Research and employ vetted curricula or seek consultation on your ideas before enacting them.

Interrogating Systems of Inequity

Teaching from texts that exclude a broad range of intersectional, cultural, and racial identities is corrosive to learning and impedes a full and critical understanding of a subject. When curriculum ignores and devalues people who share the identity and backgrounds of students, students learn that they themselves don't matter. This undercuts their ability to learn and their belief in themselves as scholars and as valuable members of society. Additionally, attempts to address inequity by focusing only on the consequence of inequity, rather than the sources of it, can exacerbate these destructive narratives. Gwendolyn D., a school psychologist and parenting expert in Philadelphia public schools, offers an example: "When designing projects about lack of resources, such as book deserts or food insecurity, it is important to encourage teachers to require students to examine systemic decisions and underlying factors that contribute to the problem. Without this, students will be left with the ineluctable conclusion that personal or group cultural failing was the cause, rather than systemic inequity."

We must adopt curricula that offers an inclusive story of history and the contributions of persons of color, women, the LGBTQ+ community, and other historically excluded populations across disciplines. Inclusive curricula must be partnered with critical pedagogy that enables students to examine systemic and institutional inequities.

Here are some approaches to interrogating systems of inequity in the classroom:

- **Examine the contemporary experiences in students' communities.** Pose larger philosophical questions, such as: *What is a good life? What are the basic needs of people?* Ask students to contemplate whether basic needs in the society are being met for all. Have them explore historic patterns in differences in power and privilege relative to need.

- **Intentionally use the language associated with discussions of inequities in society and the reasons they exist.** Ask students: *What does it mean to have power? Does privilege exist in our community? Does everyone have power? Is power unequally distributed? Is power good or bad? Do you have power or privilege and in what way(s)?*

- **In age- and developmentally appropriate ways, study violence that impacts many vulnerable communities.** Partner with behavioral health professionals, particularly social workers, to manage discussions and allow expression of feelings that can arise. Have students examine the history of war and local manifestations of violence in daily life and engage them in discussions about strategies and solutions.

- **Conduct mock elections and study the history of voting in the context of race and gender and its importance to American democracy.** Examine contemporary elections and messaging. Explore the divisive nature of politics and elections, and have students research standards for change.

- **Explore the concept of marginalization.** Examine how individuals and groups have been oppressed and highlight stories of conquering and victimization. Also, discuss stories of cultures flourishing and creating innovations and making contributions despite power imbalances in society. Ask students if they see themselves as a victim or a conqueror. Explore these concepts and how they impact identity and manifest in power imbalance in the contemporary context.

- **Discuss social change movements.** Highlight historic social movements for civil or women's rights and use these models as a basis to discuss modern movements around climate change, Black Lives Matter, and anti-gun violence efforts. Discuss strategies employed, including messaging, and evaluate success and failures of ongoing struggles. Have students generate their own ideas and potential social movement strategy.

Valuing and Activating Student Voice

Learning flourishes where students' voices and identities are valued. We educators should be steeped in local history and learn about local governments, as well as investigate the family histories, culture, and community context of the students we teach. Equity-based instruction incorporates daily teaching strategies that validate each child's cultural identities. In validating and affirming the intersectionality of how students may identify across race, gender, sexual orientation, and other affiliations, we make learning more relatable for them.

Here are some approaches to valuing and affirming the voice and identity of students, their families, and the greater community:

- **Encourage student confidence in using their voice.** Create opportunities for mock debates, but emphasize that difference in opinions must be valued and respected. Teach students how to navigate emotions associated with difference. Assign students to facilitate discussions about equity and justice matters with the class or in small groups. Have students collaborate with fellow students to generate questions to facilitate class discussion.

- **Engage in visionary justice exercises.** Create opportunities for students to read, write, or develop art or music that explores and expresses the many facets of their identities. Establish social justice literary circles in which students share opinions about books they chose for themselves that reflect people in difficult circumstances. Assign projects in which students create messages about inequity and identify how to be a change agent to overcome imbalances of power.

- **Create cooperative classroom learning opportunities to give students voice in learning.** Develop opportunities for students to learn in creative and dynamic ways. Devise guided questions to allow room for critical interaction and discussion among students about their opinions and generate individual and shared ideas of problem solving: *Are there victims in this situation? What is a victim? Is there someone exerting power in a harmful way? How might you do things differently? Are there ways in which culture protected or harmed the individuals involved? How does identity contribute to the outcome of the situations?*

- **Use reading and writing exercises to develop students' imagination in which they envision themselves as change agents.** Invite students to read science fiction on dystopian futures in which groups of people are marginalized. *Octavia's Brood,* for example, is a collection of short science-fiction stories inspired by award-winning author Octavia Butler. Challenge students to write their own dystopian short story and envision themselves as the main character who combats the oppressive power authority.

Leveraging Culture and Relevant Historical Context

Leveraging culture and authentic historical context in lesson plans is a key element of equitable instruction. When students see themselves reflected in the context of content areas, they identify new possibilities for themselves as learners and as citizens. Students must see themselves, their communities, and their culture as relevant to learning. In many cases, leveraging culture may be the key to reaching students who feel locked out of the learning process. As Craig M., a superintendent of a public charter school in Boston, Massachusetts, explains, "We might also tap into contemporary culture a student values and use it as an effective instructional device. This method paved the way for me to connect with a student who had been repeatedly left back and opened the door for him to progress."

It is not only students from historically ignored groups who suffer at the hands of perspectives that do not offer complete context and inclusive viewpoints of history. Marcela H., a White parent in New York, was concerned that the skewed focus and overemphasis on enslavement and segregation periods in history classes shaped her son's perception of Black people as downtrodden. Marcela asks, "Why was my son learning only about these difficult periods in history and not the broad range of contributions Africans from across the diaspora have made to science, math, innovation, and the arts?"

Here are some tools for leveraging culture and providing relevant historical context in instruction:

- **Identify culturally appropriate historic texts that have been widely vetted to supplement the existing textbooks and classroom resources.** In the absence of a school-wide or district-wide adaptation of curricula, there are many well-known resources that can bring equitable history into the classroom. One such resource is Howard Zinn's *A Young People's History of the United States.* Jody B., a parent from Glendale, Maryland, recommends Composer (composereducation.org), an education website for citizen education resources.

- **Use firsthand narratives when studying history.** Just as students should be encouraged to give voice to their values, beliefs, concerns, and ideas, it is essential that they learn that history is more than what is reported in the pages of a textbook. First-account narratives—such as those of enslaved people, Holocaust survivors, Black and Indigenous soldiers in World War II, civil rights activists, and contemporary refugees from Syria—breathe life into lessons and can facilitate the incorporation of knowledge as well as empathy. Always review these materials before presenting them to the class to assess whether or not they are appropriate for your students.

- **Use contemporary fiction and nonfiction texts to explore matters of social justice.** Have students examine the history of the criminal justice system and other areas of legal justice and rights—such as personal responsibility vs. collective responsibility, rights to privacy, individual vs. corporate rights, and the history of voting—through the lens of the influence of race, gender, sexual orientation, affirmative action, and religion. Bryan Stevenson, a legal social justice advocate and winner of multiple Supreme Court decisions, wrote a best-selling autobiographical book entitled *Just Mercy*. A student reader version of his book can be accessed on CommonLit (commonlit.org/en/book-pairings/just-mercy), along with tips for probing questions to analyze the text.

- **Use rap and other contemporary forms of music to explore metaphor, alliteration, and poetry.** Use classic works to expose students to the fundamentals of English language and contrast them with contemporary music in their use of literary devices. Make sure to review the lyrics first, however, for harmful language. Slam poetry is another exciting contemporary art form with which many students are familiar. Have students create their own slam poetry and have a contest or showcase of poems that highlight their daily life, musings, and/or observations about justice matters.

Promoting Student-Centered Learning

In the classroom, strong relationships between students and teachers have proven efficacious in creating a stronger, safer learning environment and establishing an atmosphere in which students feel more engaged and motivated to learn and achieve. We must teach students to self-evaluate and self-advocate. We must provide concrete ways in which they can meaningfully practice and explore using their voice and give them the language to communicate through school projects, service learning, and identity-building opportunities.

Here are some approaches to putting students at the center of their learning:

- **Emphasize project-based learning and service learning.** Project-based learning enables students to learn deeply about a topic related to justice. Challenge students to create a documentary about a social justice matter, create and write a blog on a topic of choice, or conduct interviews with key community leaders about a particular social justice matter. Encourage students to research different topics and collectively vote on a social-change project they can undertake in the community. Have students engage with a community organization or other institution to outline alternative justice action strategies and choose one or more to enact.

- **Encourage students to study the story of their own family history to make sense of their contemporary experience and link it to a historical context.** James T., a sixth-grade history and special education teacher from Prince George's County, Maryland, suggests a "history in a bag" exercise, in which students gather personal objects from home and interview family members about each object's meaning relative to family history. Have students anchor their family's personal story in a time in history and analyze the historical context of the experience.

- **Use art—such as drawings, paintings, collages, and music—as a way for students to reflect their understanding of what happened historically or what is happening currently.** Allow students to present ideas and research conclusions using art as a tool in lieu of reading and writing.

- **Raise student awareness of the communities they live in as well as neighboring communities in their region.** Ask students critical questions to help them examine the differences and help them discern why these differences exist. Are there laws, governmental, or private-enterprise policies that have contributed to these outcomes?

- **Illustrate how mathematics and scientific research and analysis methods have practical connections to daily living and influence individual and policy decision-making in government and enterprise.** Ask students to think about what mathematical questions can be posed in their daily lives. They can study practical living-wage models or census data or connect math with how it influences prices of products, sports statistics, or their family's household budget, among others. Engage students in a process of investigating what they are curious about in the world through the lens of math or science.

Activating a Critical Lens

Numerous studies demonstrate the power of critical thinking skills and how they develop if taught with intention. Encouraging students to explain their thinking and how they arrive at logical conclusions makes them better learners, says Gwen Dewar (2012). Exercises that offer students opportunities to deduce, debate, and analyze help foster critical thinking skills and promote inquisitiveness and self-confidence. Evidence suggests that adults with critical thinking skills are generally more open-minded and fair, in addition to being better equipped to face biases and prejudices honestly. Cultivating a critical lens develops the ability to establish and participate in an equitable society.

Here are some ways to develop students' critical thinking skills:

- **Create assignments to connect students with the world.** Have them read or watch global news and present information to the class. Give students prompts to examine the relationship of what is happening in another country to what is happening in the United States. *Are they connected? What are the commonalities to the American experience? What is different?*

- **Discuss political ads and social media and evaluate commercial advertisements.** Enable students to critically analyze and think about messaging and the intention and motivation underlying the media. Ask students: *What trends do you see? What strategies do you see consistently employed? Is the message effective? Why or why not? When reading or watching these modes of communication, what emotions do they evoke? Are you persuaded? Why or why not?*

- **Have students scrutinize imagery in culture and examine the concept of cultural imperialism.** Explore the idea that one culture tends to dominate across communication and cultural platforms, including entertainment. Review how this happens, not only across the United States, but across the globe. Use local, national, and international digital media to discuss the messaging of what is beautiful or who is good or bad. Challenge students to examine trends: *What messages are being sent through these platforms about what to fear?* Connect it with research on the impact on the individual and group psyche.

- **Pose a series of philosophical questions to expand critical thinking.** For example: *Why do we need art? What purpose does education serve? What is philosophy and what purpose does it serve?*

- **Examine the different structures that comprise the American system and other global societies.** Ask students: *What are the economic structures in a society? Why are there socioeconomic divisions? Why are people in poverty? What is individual responsibility and what is collective responsibility? What are systems? What are institutions? How is it that they have power and influence the lives of people in a society?*

- **Explore the history of education.** Discuss its purpose. Look at laws and policies that have been implemented over time to suggest how and where people obtain education. Examine the contemporary context of schools, including demographics of school populations. Help students evaluate and understand school systems and the allocation of resources to support them.

Sparking Equity-Based Citizenship

Students learn citizenship behavior in school with messages that teach them to be compliant, follow rules, and not challenge authority. Such messages, however, often run counter to the critical thinking, problem solving, and questioning that is required for students to evolve into citizens who are equipped to actualize an equitable society. Good citizens may not always be compliant. Injustice in the greater society demands that we question authority and act as independent thinkers with the confidence to give voice to our concerns or to advocate for others. Moreover, governance and leadership require proactive engagement in processing divergent viewpoints. We need to provide projects and other learning opportunities that strengthen the school-community connection so students can engage with grassroots organizations, local government, and nonprofit human service organizations, as well as private enterprise. This exposure will help deepen students' understanding of how their community works and enable them to envision themselves as future leaders.

Here are some approaches to spark equity-based citizenship:

- **Develop persuasive argument units that synthesize equity and justice issues.** Have students write letters and send them to local or school authorities who might respond to or address a real-world problem students have observed.

- **Conduct Model UN programs around global issues so students can research, learn, and debate real global issues and generate alternative problem-solving strategies.** Incorporate treaties and examine global alliances for common good, such as climate-change pacts.

- **In math and science, create data-informed change agents.** Help students recognize that they can use information and data insights to research and inform policy. Teach students how to research public data sets, overlay and analyze data, and draw conclusions. Have students relate their research to larger questions that data might reveal about disparities and differences that relate to race, religion, gender, and so on.

- **Investigate policies that impact the local community.** Connect with civic, governmental, or nonprofit organizations to investigate policies and avenues for influencing change. Create a project-based learning opportunity for students to connect with these partners for research and analysis. Have them devise their own policy response and submit to a relevant individual or institutional authority for consideration.

- **Connect science with contemporary experience and historic trends.** Examine national and global government decision-making as well as individual decisions and their impact on the environment and climate change. Have students investigate water issues and environmental pollution and examine how their or neighboring communities may or may not be impacted.

Engaging Families

Equity-based instruction goes beyond the four walls of the classroom. Educators must operate on the assumption that all families want their children to succeed in school. Limiting family check-ins to report-card periods is insufficient for building relationships with caregivers and bridging school and at-home learning.

Suzanne A., a university administrator and DEI (diversity, equity, and inclusion) expert from State College, Pennsylvania, and former clinical social worker with families, notes,

Partner with caregivers in supporting their child's learning process at home.

"Teachers and administrators must understand some caregivers are focused on addressing basic living needs and survival. We must set easily attainable goals for family involvement."

Schools should seek coaching support on strategies to enhance the home and school learning connection available from providers of professional development training for educators. Beyond school-guided initiatives, we must create consistent and meaningful relationships with families and caregivers and engage them proactively in the learning process throughout the school year.

> "In the Title I school I worked in, parents did not know how to be involved. We need to describe a myriad of opportunities for parents to be engaged."
>
> —MONAI P., teacher, Virginia public schools

Here are some approaches for building relationships with families year-round:

- **Find creative ways to communicate with families and caregivers.** Connect over digital platforms, such as Zoom, to accommodate caregivers who have to work or have transportation or child-care issues. Use community-based newsletters to advertise school events or communicate classroom goals.
- **Plan brown-bag dinner opportunities twice a year to connect and discuss specific ways caregivers can support learning at home.**
- **Connect with community-based organizations that can support learning.**

Classroom Equity Plans

Classrooms are incubators for change. Teachers have the power to instruct students in a manner that creates a more equitable society, but it is essential that the instruction be structured and intentional so that its impact can be recorded, measured, replicated, improved, and broadened. Educators committed to equity and inclusion without institutional support can still incorporate intentional change in the classroom. They have control over community building, classroom management and discipline, fair grading, and relationship building with families and students. If institutional support is available at the school or district level, teachers can volunteer their classrooms to be models or places where new strategies can be piloted.

Activating the Vision

National Youth Poet Laureate Amanda Gorman (2021) eloquently reminds us in her poem "The Hill We Climb" that we are far from achieving the just society we proclaim we represent. Horace Mann's quote from the beginning of this essay positions the American education system as our best opportunity to climb "the hill" Gorman aptly describes. Gorman paves the path up the hill by examining our American "inheritance" and filtering it through a critical lens. It reveals that we can aspire for more. It recognizes that the work of reviewing and repairing the past can guide us to fully actualize our great society. Equity in education can be achieved by relevant, consistent, and consequential activities and actions implemented by individual teachers who are committed to creating an equitable and just learning experience in the classroom and beyond.

Celeste M. Bryant, MSW, is a strategic planning consultant and social justice community organizer in the greater Washington, D.C., area. She has devoted her career to galvanizing public and private partnerships to address the needs of vulnerable populations. As a Scholastic consultant, Bryant promotes professional development and classroom strategies for K–12 educators. Her history with public middle schools, fostering social health and skills development to encourage academic achievement, informs her current work dedicated to promoting equity in the classroom. Bryant is a certified expert in Cultural Competence and is a former adjunct faculty member at the University of Pennsylvania Graduate School of Social Work, where she taught courses in institutionalized racism and social change and social movements. She currently leads social justice efforts to build Black equity and wealth through home ownership in Washington, D.C.

Maximizing Field Trips to Close Opportunity Gaps

by Tai Jones

Many of us still hold the memory of special field trips taken throughout our school days—for me, it was a trip to the Coca-Cola Bottling Company. From the moment the bus pulled into the facility's driveway, I became excited about seeing all the various memorabilia, the polar bears, the countless items on which the Coca-Cola brand is featured (lunchboxes were my favorite), and the swirl of all the cascading bottles being filled. Knowing that at the end of our facility tour, we would each savor a chilled, bottle-capped mini-Coke of our own on the picnic grounds made the trip extra special. In hindsight, the tour of the facility was meant to be an enrichment activity to level the playing field for a very diverse class of students. Most of the students were Black or Brown and lived in poverty; they were bussed into a neighborhood that their families could not afford to live in.

While field trips can help level the playing field, they are not always equitably distributed. An article published in the *Bethesda Beat* reported that Montgomery County Schools acknowledged "inequities in their student field trips" (Peetz, 2019).

Although the district ensured all elementary schools participated in a minimum of one field trip, upper grade levels were not bound by the same guidelines. Even in their comparison of two elementary schools with enrollment of about 700 students each, one campus arranged 43 field trips, while the other arranged only four that year. The school with the fewer field trips has a free- or reduced-lunch population of about 81 percent. School board member Pat O'Neil said, "That is a problem because field trips enrich what happens in the classroom; finding [a] level playing field is important."

Students of every background need ongoing, consistent championed opportunity growth, equitable distribution of district resources, equitable pathways to achievement, and fostered inclusion. In her article, "The Opportunity Gap: Extracurriculars and Field Trips Aren't Just for Fun," Jessica Poiner states: "Extracurricular activities are a powerful tool for closing the opportunity gap" (2015). She notes Robert Putnam, who pointed out in his book, *Our Kids: The American Dream in Crisis*, that extracurricular activities were "invented in American schools, by social reformers, for the purpose of training kids in what we now call soft skills" (2016). When planning such activities for all our students, we educators have to be certain that there is a BIG picture approach to how we design and execute holistically equitable learning opportunities. Field trips provide a trifecta combination of hands-on learning (even virtually), sightseeing, and travel. Additionally, these trips expand cognitive development in children because they are afforded the opportunity to actualize their studies and creativity in real life.

Equity Exposure: Children Learn What They Live . . .

Reared in a God-fearing, middle-class African American home, my parents and their parents always believed our life's journey could pendulum from the Louisiana backwoods to the suburbs. Affectionately, my grandmother hailed the adage "from the outhouse to the White House," and vehemently believed we should be exposed to all the things that would give us a well-rounded education and prepare us to meet opportunity when presented with it. In the same vein as my grandmother, Dorothy Law Nolte's poem, "Children Learn What They Live," has been a guidepost for me to always acknowledge the needs of each student who walks into the classroom. The bigger promise of what children can dream themselves to be can only exist when they see, believe, and are shaped into beings destined to have more opportunity than the previous generation.

Instructionally, the best field trips—whether virtual or in-person—enrich learning impacts and embrace inclusivity while developing a student's critical thinking skills. When I moved into a large urban district and mentored students, I received a quick lesson that systemic social dependence and survival could be found within a five-mile radius of a students' residence. I also learned that an affinity for one's community can morph into captivity from lack of exposure. I am reminded of an 8-year-old student who was totally incapable of distinguishing his neighborhood in the southern sector from another neighborhood in the northern sector of the same city. Yes, the two neighborhoods were vastly different, but his

Field trips enrich learning and develop students' critical thinking skills.

confusion was a result of limited exposure outside of his own neighborhood. He was unable to see the differences in resources: owning a family vehicle versus riding the bus or a train or living in a home instead of a high-rise or basement apartment. However, when our preparation included an equity lens, augmented by a city map, things that were seemingly unrelated but familiar to him became an extension of what he came to know as "his" community.

Well-designed equitable field trips will bridge multiple subjects, combine learning needs, and consider the needs of the highest-performing student as well as struggling students. In small rural districts, field trips can be targeted in lower grades to visit a college or university to propel a continuum of higher education. Strengthening observation skills by an immersion into sensory activities creates active and engaged learners who are experiential learning participants.

Equity Field Trips: The Connection to Learning

Not only do field trips enrich what happens in the classroom, they can shape students' futures. The U.S. Travel Association conducted a study of 400 adults balanced for gender, age, race, and income. Half of the respondents had taken at least one educational trip between the ages of 12 and 18, the other half had not. The study found that regardless of gender, ethnicity, or socioeconomic status, students who take educational trips have better grades (59 percent) and higher high school graduation rates (95 percent), go on to college (63 percent), and receive greater income (12 percent higher annually). Even more revealing to the lifelong impact, 89 percent indicated educational trips as having a positive, lasting impact on their education and career. They believed the trips made them more intellectually curious and encouraged continuous engagement beyond the classroom (NEA, n.d.).

Beyond a doubt, educational equity has been difficult to achieve in classrooms, and by no means is a field trip alone going to end the disparity that exists in student households all over the country. However, field trips do provide each student with exposure opportunities. They expose students to places outside their socioeconomic status and to possibilities, opportunities, careers, new ways of thinking, and new expectations. Field trips help students dream and think big. David C. Banks, New York City Schools chancellor and founding principal of the Eagle Academy Foundation, shared a visionary's approach to assure equitable outcomes for students from any background. In his 2016 opening speech during the Democratic National Convention, he spoke to the fact that "addressing the crisis facing [children] of color in our country [requires] innovative measures." Field trips are a powerful, innovative tool that can bridge the equity gap for students who don't have a variety of experiences or exposures in their community. As Banks has said, "It's hard to dream of being an investment banker if you've never met one."

Your plan for a field trip must be relevant to the dynamics of your student population, must engage students with the curriculum-based topics taught in the classroom, and should be used strategically within your lesson plans.

Prior to the pandemic, the joy of field trips had succumbed to problems of funding, student liability issues, complaints of lost instructional time, and the view that it was a waste of school district time and resources. However, when the world changed, so did our overall perspective of the need to transform student learning. As educators both in classrooms and households, we can all attest to the importance of complementing traditional teaching and learning with meaningful alternatives that add value to all students' education.

Whether teaching in a virtual, hybrid, or brick-and-mortar space, your plan for a field trip must be relevant to the dynamics of your student population, must engage students with the curriculum-based topics taught in the classroom, and should be used strategically within your lesson plans. A review in the *International Journal of Environmental and Science Education* credits teachers who have learned how to develop and orchestrate successful field trips with preplanning, implementation, and the ability to reflect within their lessons as direct influencers of their students (Behrendt & Franklin, 2014). Although many teachers like converting their classrooms into virtual havens to explore and deepen their educational knowledge with hands-on visuals, they realize field trips require proper planning and preparation. Goal-focused field trips should emphasize an equitable component for all populations served by its audience. To ensure there is a measurement rubric, equitable approaches should recognize that some students—because of race, social status, or other special needs—benefit from more help than others to achieve their goals.

Students benefit from field trips that expose them to experiences outside their community.

Your plan for a field trip should help students build awareness; recognize and work around their opportunity gap; and inspire continued momentum after the field trip and into their lifetimes.

Level Up: Field Trips Close Equity Opportunity Gaps

Tetyana Denford, a freelance writer for *Elle* and *Vogue* magazines, penned a letter to her small-town high school teacher thanking him for a field trip to New York City that he sponsored for her graduating class of 20. She wrote: "That one experience gave us the answers to the inevitable question we would ask ourselves as adults—how do I want to be? Not '*what* do I want to be', but *how*. *How* is connected to the way we perceive the world, and our place in it, and this will ultimately give us the tools to shape our future."

Field trips provide an opportunity for students to see the world in a new real-life connected way, offering cultural connections and a greater relationship to one's own dreams and ambitions. With that goal in mind, Act One, an organization based in Arizona, has, for more than 10 years, provided hundreds of thousands of students from Title I schools access to live performances, theatre, museums, and music throughout Tucson and Phoenix. Act One believes that "arts education has the ability to take students beyond the standard classroom environment through active and engaged learning practices and is an essential component of a well-rounded education."

Virtual Field Trips: Adventures at Your Fingertips

Although the pandemic and funding sources have limited district resources for field trips, virtual tours remain available through both private, for-profit professional tour companies and countless free resources. If you are in a district where students are asked to pay for field trips, you might consider keeping virtual field trips as an option even after the pandemic. It can help lessen the financial burden and expand the opportunity growth for students who may not have the financial means to pay for in-person field trips.

Plan your virtual field trips by reaching out to organizations of interest; some have prepared lessons plans and guided offerings that allow students to have an interactive visit. Additionally, as you plan your field trips with an equity focus for all students, remember to expand the discussion with literature from your classroom or school library. To find companion books for your field trips, go to clubs.scholastic.com/bookfinder.

Below is a list of just some of the virtual tours available. The list is divided into four categories: Science, Art, History and Culture, and Other (virtual tours that provide a variety of learning experiences in several subject areas). Note: All URLs are current as of this book's printing. However, be sure to check them before sending students to the websites to ensure they are still working as intended.

SCIENCE

American Museum of Natural History https://www.amnh.org/calendar
New York City's AMNH suggests several options for virtual visits, including virtual field trips, an "inside the museum" high-resolution picture tour, guided tours on Facebook Live, and an expedition app experience that includes quizzes and exhibit highlights.

Boston Museum of Science https://www.mos.org/explore/mos-at-home
Boston's premier science museum presents a Museum of Science at Home experience, consisting of virtual exhibits, daily livestreams, podcasts, town halls, and family STEM activities. The museum provides digital programs for both adults and children, with highlights including live social events, an ant colony webcam, and stimulating multimedia content.

Cincinnati Zoo https://cincinnatizoo.org/home-safari-resources
The Cincinnati Zoo offers a home safari consisting of videos recorded during Facebook Live streams. Website visitors can browse more than 50 animal encounters and learn facts about creatures, such as red pandas, parrots, zebras,

and orangutans. Online modules also include activities, such as homemade birdfeeders and balancing exercises so kids can participate more fully in the virtual experience.

Maryland Zoo https://www.marylandzoo.org/animals/live-cams-feeds
The Maryland Zoo hosts five live webcams: penguins, flamingos, lions, giraffes, and elephants, and include giraffe and penguin feeding.

Monterey Bay Aquarium
https://www.montereybayaquarium.org/animals/live-cams
California's Monterey Bay Aquarium hosts ten live webcams featuring critters such as penguins, jellyfish, sharks, and sea otters. The variety of exhibits means that teachers can switch among streams when a particular camera is not live. The aquarium also facilitates narrated feeding times on certain webcams during weekdays, with the feeding schedule posted on the site.

National Aquarium https://aqua.org and https://aqua.org/explore/livestreams
The National Aquarium in Baltimore hosts three 24/7 webcam livestreams and offers guided virtual programs as well.

The National Museum of the United States Air Force
https://www.nationalmuseum.af.mil/Visit/Virtual-Tour
The National Museum of the United States Air Force, near Dayton, Ohio, provides digital resources, such as 360-degree photo cockpit tours, podcasts, and videos. The site also supplies lesson plans broken down by grade level, with extra resources, including aircraft coloring pages and word searches.

Oregon Zoo https://www.oregonzoo.org/discover/virtual-encounters
The Oregon Zoo offers virtual encounters on platforms such as Zoom, Microsoft Teams, and GoToMeeting. During these sessions, animals, such as armadillos, giraffes, elephants, sloths, and lemurs, along with their caregivers join virtual visitors for a 15-minute meet and greet. The two available daily time slots are at 10 am and 2 pm Pacific Time.

Space Center Houston https://spacecenter.org/resources
Space Center Houston offers free interactive virtual learning experiences, including an online *Apollo 13* exhibit, video series, and an app that offers mobile tours plus augmented reality and virtual reality experiences. The center also occasionally hosts virtual stargazing campouts and suggests at-home science experiments and games. Plus, the website features a wealth of online outer space resources.

ART

Art Institute of Chicago https://www.artic.edu/visit-us-virtually
The Art Institute of Chicago facilitates online visits consisting of virtual video and audio tours, searchable online collections, and digital publications, as well as online lesson plans and art projects. There is even an Ask an Educator form that enables parents or teachers to communicate with museum staff who handpick resources to assist with lessons planning.

Frida Kahlo Museum
https://www.museofridakahlo.org.mx/en/the-blue-house/virtual-tour
The virtual tour of the Frida Kahlo Museum in Mexico City is one of the most colorful museum tours online. Virtual visitors explore various areas of the grounds in a 360-degree, up-close experience. The colors of the architecture and artifacts are works of art in themselves and are sure to brighten viewers' days. The website offers additional resources, including downloadable photos, videos, quotes, and even recipes.

J. Paul Getty Museum
https://artsandculture.google.com/partner/the-j-paul-getty-museum
The Google Arts & Culture online tour of the Getty Museum spans dozens of exhibits with thousands of digital artifacts. Pieces date as far back as the eighth century and up to modern times, with notable works of art, including *The Virgin Mary with Saints Thomas Aquinas and Paul, Rembrandt Laughing,* and *Irises.*

The Metropolitan Museum of Art
https://www.metmuseum.org/art/online-features/met-360-project and https://www.metmuseum.org/art/art-at-home
The Met 360° Project is a collection of six wide-lens videos compatible with both virtual reality systems and regular computer screens or smartphones. Virtual viewers take a point-of-view tour of museum areas, such as the Great Hall, the Met Cloisters, and the Arms and Armor Gallery, set to a soundtrack of instrumental music. The Met website also hosts an Art at Home series that offers up-close, virtual access and analysis of famous works, as well as videos of conservation projects and instructions for art projects.

Musée du Louvre https://www.louvre.fr/en/online-tours
A virtual tour from Paris's Louvre consists of 360-degree panoramic views of exhibit halls, such as Egyptian Antiquities and the ruins of the Louvre Moat. With a special app, visitors can also experience the *Mona Lisa* in virtual reality. The museum website hosts multimedia online exhibitions of famous works, such as *Portrait of the Marquise de Pompadour* and *Psyche Revived by Cupid's Kiss.*

Museu de Arte de São Paulo

https://artsandculture.google.com/exhibit/art-from-italy-from-rafael-to-titian/KwJinoW1KLg0Lg

MASP has an impressive online presence with more than 1,000 images of paintings, photographs, and objects in its Google Arts & Culture collection. Online visitors can delve into South American art and culture by exploring exhibits and browsing through digital collections. The Google app also enables virtual reality tours of the museum via smartphone.

Museum of Modern Art https://www.moma.org/calendar/groups/58

New York City's MoMA launched a virtual views series, which enables website visitors to browse rotating online exhibits. MoMA also hosts virtual events with components, such as live Q&A sessions with artists and curators, readings and theatrical performances, 3-D renderings, and interactive games.

National Museum of Australia https://www.nma.gov.au/learn/digital-outreach

Australia's national museum offers free one-hour digital excursions to schools that cannot visit the museum in person. The tours are available on weekdays by request and accommodate groups of 10 to 30 students. Classes meet with museum staff via Zoom and complete missions based on themes, such as the fight for Indigenous rights. Virtual exhibition gallery tours are also available.

National Museum of Modern and Contemporary Art, Korea

https://artsandculture.google.com/partner/national-museum-of-modern-and-contemporary-art-korea

Google's online tour of Korea's National Museum of Modern and Contemporary Art enables web visitors to explore the country's unique culture and heritage. The tour includes multiple online exhibits, hundreds of pieces of modern artwork, and several floors of the building, including sections of the outdoor sculpture garden.

Solomon R. Guggenheim Museum

https://www.guggenheim.org/group-visits#digitalprograms

The Guggenheim offers staff-facilitated online tours for students from kindergarten to grade 12. Educators can book interactive, real-time tours for classes that engage students and enable question-and-answer sessions. Tours are free for New York City public schools. For other districts, the tours are $75 per hour, and discounted rates are available. Tours have a maximum of 30 participants, so groups are sure to receive an intimate experience.

HISTORY & CULTURE

9/11 Memorial & Museum
https://www.911memorial.org/visit/about-your-visit/learn-and-explore-home
New York City's 9/11 Memorial & Museum website has a learn-and-explore feature that includes live, guide-led panoramic virtual tours of the rebuilt trade center, interactive videos, and webinar stories. The site also recommends activities to do at home with children to simulate the museum's activity stations.

Anne Frank House https://www.annefrank.org/en/museum/web-and-digital
The Anne Frank House in Amsterdam welcomes visitors from around the world with digital experiences, such as video, virtual reality, 360-degree photos of the Frank home, and translations of the diary in over 20 languages. Virtual visitors can also browse a pocket gallery by downloading the app.

Palace Museum and the Forbidden City
https://en.dpm.org.cn/multimedia/virutual/ and https://www.youvisit.com/tour/chinatour/100444
The Palace Museum sits in the heart of Beijing, China, and houses centuries' worth of art and history. The museum building is a monument to classic Chinese architecture, as is the surrounding palace complex, the Forbidden City. Virtual visitors can tour works inside the museum and stroll through the outer courtyards by indulging in interactive and immersive virtual and VR tours. Both options give viewers the opportunity to explore the grounds up close without navigating the crowds.

Pergamonmuseum
https://artsandculture.google.com/partner/pergamonmuseum-staatliche-museen-zu-berlin
Berlin's Pergamonmuseum contains a wealth of art and archaeological treasures, and curators give home viewers a glimpse into the collections through several online exhibits on Google Arts & Culture. The collection includes over 1,000 images of objects made of clay, metal, copper, and gemstone, originating in regions such as Iran, Spain, Turkey, and Germany.

The Strong National Museum of Play
https://artsandculture.google.com/partner/the-strong
The Strong Museum in Rochester, New York, examines the history of playtime throughout recent history. Its online exhibits follow fun themes, such as Pinball in America, the History of Valentines, and Oregon Trail computer games.

United States Holocaust Memorial Museum
https://www.ushmm.org/teach/teaching-materials/primary-sources-collections/virtual-field-trip
The United States Holocaust Memorial Museum offers virtual museum tours for students. The self-guided digital tour highlights virtual scenes from nine

museum areas, such as Hall of Witness and the Hall of Remembrance, as well as the Holocaust exhibit. The site also offers free teacher resources and lesson materials, including a worksheet with an answer key.

Vatican Museums
https://www.museivaticani.va/content/museivaticani/en/collezioni/musei/tour-virtuali-elenco.html
The Vatican Museums provide an online experience consisting of 360-degree high-resolution photos of over a dozen features, such as the Sistine Chapel and Raphael's Rooms. The website also grants web access to archaeological areas, various departments, and a searchable online catalog.

OTHER

Boston Children's Museum
https://www.bostonchildrensmuseum.org/learning-resources
The Boston Children's Museum provides learning resources, including weekly activity emails, Mad Libs, and links to mini digital museums and interactive apps, keeping kids occupied for hours.

Children's Museum Houston https://www.cmhouston.org/virtual-field-trips
The Children's Museum Houston provides regular content, such as 3-D digital field trips, virtual adventure camps, daily broadcasted project tutorials, webinar workshops, and video call-in shows. The museum also has a free smartphone app for additional at-home adventures.

Children's Museum Indianapolis
https://www.childrensmuseum.org/museum-at-home
Children's Museum Indianapolis provides an at-home museum experience, including ongoing virtual events, digital museum programs, follow-along hands-on activities, and virtual birthday parties. The museum also creates holiday-themed downloadable activity bundles and resources for teachers.

National Parks Service
https://www.nps.gov/subjects/npscelebrates/find-your-virtual-park.htm
The NPS offers virtual tours of several national parks. Students can learn about history, science, art, and more. Some tours include videos, webcams, photos, and multimedia galleries. In addition to these virtual learning opportunities, NPS also offers live virtual events happening at national parks across the country, podcasts, and video and photo tours.

Smithsonian Institution https://www.si.edu/museums

The Smithsonian has a number of museums with a plethora of learning experiences for students. For example:

- National Museum of Natural History offers a self-guided virtual tour of current and past museum exhibits.

- National Portrait Gallery, America's Presidents, is the nation's only complete collection of presidential portraits outside the White House. It includes workshops and programs for young people and Portrait Discovery Kits for kids and families.

- National Museum of African American History and Culture is the largest and most comprehensive museum in the nation where all Americans can learn about the richness and diversity of the African American history and culture.

- National Museum of the American Indian focuses on advancing knowledge of Native cultures of the western hemisphere.

Tai Jones has worked in the educational publishing industry for more than 17 years and has received numerous accolades from several sales and community service organizations. As an educator, journalist, author, and community servant, she harnessed a love of providing equality and equity solutions for underserved populations. She is a proud member of The Links, Inc., the Cahn Fellows Advisory Board, and NABSE, and is a recipient of the Scholastic Education President's Award. A Louisiana native, Jones makes her home in the state of Texas, where she lives near her mother, three nephews, sister, and brother-in-law, and a host of relatives and friends.

Select References

"The Pursuit of Equity in Education" (page 8)

Alsaleh, N. J. (2020). Teaching critical thinking: A literature review. *Turkish Online Journal of Educational Technology, 19*(1), 21–39. https://eric.ed.gov/?id=EJ1239945

Center for Excellence in Learning and Teaching (CELT), Iowa State University. (2017). *Revised Bloom's Taxonomy.* https://www.celt.iastate.edu/teaching/effective-teaching-practices/revised-blooms-taxonomy

Center for University Teaching, Learning, and Assessment (CUTLA), University of West Florida. (2015). *Revised Bloom's Taxonomy Chart.* https://www.acenet.edu/Documents/Blooms-Taxonomy-Chart.pdf

Collins, R. (2014). Skills for the 21st century: Teaching higher order thinking. *Curriculum & Leadership Journal, 12*(14). http://www.curriculum.edu.au/leader/teaching_higher_order_thinking,37431.html

Dobbie, W. & Fryer, R. G. Jr. (2011). Are high-quality schools enough to increase achievement among the poor? Evidence from the Harlem Children's Zone. *American Economic Journal: Applied Economics, 3*(3), 158–187. http://www.aeaweb.org/articles.php?doi=10.1257/app.3.3.158

Dodge, B. (2017). *WebQuest lesson template.* Webquest. https://webquest.org/sdsu/templates/lesson-template1.htm

Echeverria, J. & Short, D. (2000). *Using multiple perspectives in observations of diverse classrooms: The Sheltered Instruction Observation Protocol (SIOP).* https://eric.ed.gov/?id=ED441334

Edmonds, R. (1979). *Effective schools for the urban poor.* Association for Supervision and Curriculum Development. https://www.ascd.org/el/articles/effective-schools-for-the-urban-poor

Gates, S. (2018, October 18). *Benefits of collaboration.* National Educational Association. https://www.nea.org/professional-excellence/student-engagement/tools-tips/benefits-collaboration

Green, J. & McAward, J. M. (2021). *Common interpretation: The Thirteenth Amendment.* Interactive Constitution. https://constitutioncenter.org/interactive-constitution/interpretation/amendment-xiii/interps/137

Hale, J. (2019, July 24). *The Supreme Court decision that kept suburban schools segregated.* The Conversation. https://theconversation.com/the-supreme-court-decision-that-kept-suburban-schools-segregated-120478

Interactive Constitution. (2021). *14th amendment: Citizenship rights, equal protection, apportionment, Civil War debt.* https://constitutioncenter.org/interactive-constitution/amendment/amendment-xiv

Interactive Constitution. (2021). *15th amendment: Right to vote not denied by race.* https://constitutioncenter.org/interactive-constitution/amendment/amendment-xv

Italiano, L. (March 18, 2021). Thousands call for teacher who had student clean clogged toilet with bare hands to be fired. *New York Post.* https://nypost.com/2021/03/18/arkansas-teacher-made-5-year-old-boy-clean-toilet-bare-handed-to-teach-him-a-lesson

Ladson-Billings, G. (2009). The *Dreamkeepers: Successful teachers of African American children* (2nd ed.). Jossey-Bass.

Lewin, K. (2015). *Principles of topological psychology.* Martino Fine Books.

Lunenburg, F. C. (2010). Schools as open systems. *Schooling, 1*(1), p. 1–5. http://www.nationalforum.com/Electronic Journal Volumes/Lununburg, Fred C. Schools as Open Systems Schooling V1 N1 2010.pdf

Lynch, M. (2017, May 9). *Pass or fail: Horace Mann—An American public school pioneer.* The Edvocate. https://www.theedadvocate.org/horace-mann-an-education-pioneer

MacLean, N. (2018). *Democracy in chains.* Penguin Books.

National Board for Professional Teaching Standards (2021). *Five core propositions.* https://www.nbpts.org/certification/five-core-propostions

National Humanities Center. (2006). *Of servants and slaves in Virginia, 1705.* http://nationalhumanitiescenter.org/pds/amerbegin/power/text8/BeverlyServSlaves.pdf

National Park Service. (n.d.). *In the words of others ... Enactment of the hereditary slavery law Virginia 1662–Act XII.* https://www.nps.gov/ethnography/aah/aaheritage/Chesapeake_pop2.htm

Nelson, K. M. & Bell, E. D. (2012). Addressing the needs of English language learners. In J. Etim, *Essays in helping diverse learners attain educational success.* The Edwin Mellen Press.

Noguera, P. (2019, April). Why school integration matters. *Educational Leadership, 76*(7). 20–28. https://eric.ed.gov/?id=EJ1211791

Otterman, S. (2010, October 10). Lauded Harlem schools have their own problem. *The New York Times.* https://www.nytimes.com/2010/10/13/education/13harlem.html

Powell, F. D., Fields, L. D., Bell, E. D., Johnson, G. S. (2007). Manhood, scholarship, perseverance, uplift, and elementary students: An example of school and community collaboration. *Urban Education, 42*(4), 296–312. https://www.learntechlib.org/p/100801/

Ravenscroft, S. P., Buckless, F. A., & Hassall, T. (1999). Cooperative learning – a literature guide. *Accounting Education, 8*(2), 163–176. https://www.tandfonline.com/doi/abs/10.1080/096392899330991?journalCode=raed20

Slavin, R. E. & Oickle, E. (1981, July). Effects of cooperative learning teams on student achievement and race relations: Treatment by race interactions. *Sociology of Education, 54*(3), 174–180. https://doi.org/10.2307/2112329

Urofsky, M. I. (n.d.). Dred Scott decision. *Encyclopedia Britannica.* https://www.britannica.com/event/Dred-Scott-decision

Wang, M. C., Haertel, G. D., Walberg, H. J. (1993). What helps students learn? Spotlight on student success. *Educational Leadership,* December 1993/January 1994, 74–79. https://eric.ed.gov/?id=ED461694

Weick, K. E. (1976). Educational organizations as loosely coupled systems. *Administrative Science Quarterly, 21*(1), 1–19. https://doi.org/10.2307/2391875

Winston-Salem/Forsyth County Schools. (2021). *Policy Code: 1100 Equity.* https://boardpolicyonline.com/bl/?b=forsyth#&&hs=786175

"The Powerful Promise of an Equitable Early Childhood Education" (page 21)

Children's Defense Fund. (1995). *A time for courage and truth.* http://childrensdefense.org

Donaldson, M., Grieve, R., & Pratt, J. (1983). *Early childhood development and education: Readings in psychology.* Blackwell Publishers.

Fulghum, R. (2004). *All I really need to know I learned in kindergarten* (25th anniversary edition). Ballantine.

Imaginable Futures. (2020, August). *Learning reimagined: Radical thinking for equitable futures.* https://www.imaginablefutures.com/learning-reimagined

Mayo Clinic. (2021). *Child development: Know what's ahead.* https://www.mayoclinic.org/healthy-lifestyle/childrens-health/in-depth/child-development/art-20045155

Missouri's Early Care & Education. (2019). *Early connections: Child health and development.* https://earlyconnections.mo.gov/professionals/child-health-development

National Center for Educational Statistics. (2017). *Compulsory school attendance laws, minimum and maximum age limits for required free education, by state: 2017.* https://nces.ed.gov/programs/statereform/tab5_1.asp

"Building Equity Through Collective Teacher Efficacy" (page 32)

California Department of Education. (2021). *Multi-tiered system of supports.* https://www.cde.ca.gov/ci/cr/ri

Donohoo, J. (2016). *Collective efficacy: How educators' beliefs impact student learning.* Corwin.

Gay, G. (2018). *Culturally responsive teaching: Theory, research, and practice* (3rd ed.). Teachers College Press.

Hammond, Z. (2014). *Culturally responsive teaching and the brain: Promoting authentic engagement and rigor among culturally and linguistically diverse students.* Corwin.

Hattie, J. (2012). *Visible learning for teachers: Maximizing impact on learning.* Routledge.

Hollie, S. (2017). *Culturally and linguistically responsive teaching and learning: Classroom practices for student success* (2nd ed.). Shell Education.

Ladson-Billings, G. (2009). *The dreamkeepers: Successful teachers of African American children* (2nd ed.). Jossey-Bass.

Thomas B. Fordham Institute. (2021, March 23). *The acceleration imperative: A plan to address elementary students' unfinished learning in the wake of Covid-19.* https://fordhaminstitute.org/national/research/acceleration-imperative-plan-address-elementary-students-unfinished-learning-wake

"Seeing and Teaching the Whole Child" (page 45)

Brown, F. E. & Murray, E. T. (2005). Essentials of literacy: From a pilot site at Davis Street school to district-wide intervention. *Journal of Education for Students Placed at Risk, 10*(2), 185–197.

Comer, J., Giordano, L. & Brown, F. (2012). Integrating six developmental pathways in the classroom: The synergy between teacher and student. In P. M. Brown, M. W. Corrigan, & A. Higgins-D'Alessandro (Eds.), *Handbook of prosocial education* (pp. 445–458). Rowman & Littlefield Publishers.

Dweck, C. S. (2007). *Mindset: The new psychology of success.* Ballantine.

Eugene, A. R. & Masiak, J. (2015). The neuroprotective aspects of sleep. *MEDtube science, 3*(1), 35–40. https://www.ncbi.nlm.nih.gov/pmc/articles/PMC4651462

McGonigal, K. (2014, February 13–15). *Willpower: The new science of supporting self-control, focus and resilience.* [Conference session]. Learning & the Brain Conference, San Francisco, CA. https://www.learningandthebrain.com/conference-240/teaching-self-aware-minds

Pierson, R. (2013). *Every kid needs a champion.* TED Talks Education. https://www.ted.com/talks/rita_pierson_every_kid_needs_a_champion

"Promoting High Student Achievement" (page 58)

Green, R. L. (Ed.). (2009). *Expectations in education: Readings on high expectations, effective teaching, and student achievement.* SRA/McGraw Hill.

Green, R. L. (2014). *Expect the most, provide the best.* Scholastic.

Henderson, A. T., Mapp, K. L., Johnson, V. R., & Davies, D. (2007). *Beyond the bake sale: The essential guide to family/school partnerships.* New Press.

Horbec, D. (2012, September). The link between reading and academic success. *English in Australia, 47*(2), 58–67. https://eric.ed.gov/?id=EJ998334

Redding, S. (2011). The school community: Working together for student success. In S. Redding, M. Murphy, & P. Sheley (Eds.), *Handbook on family and community engagement.* Information Age Publishing.

Scholastic FACE. (2013). *Make every student count: How collaboration among families, schools, and communities ensures student success.* https://teacher.scholastic.com/products/face/pdf/research-compendium/Compendium.pdf

Stearns, K. E. (2017). *Relationships between self-concept, teacher expectation, and academic achievement: An analysis of social-emotional well being and its relation to classroom performance.* Unpublished certificate of advanced study thesis, Sacred Heart University, Fairfield, CT. Retrieved from http://digitalcommons.sacredheart.edu/edl/19

"Recognizing and Erasing Classroom Inequity" (page 64)

Bassoff, T. C. (2005). *Adjust your teaching styles for English language learners (ELL) in ESL/Bilingual classrooms.* Teachers Network. http://www.teachersnetwork.org/ntol/howto/eslclass/tocsummit.htm

Fontaine, S. (2010, March 9). EULOGY: Thoughts on the death of Biggie Smalls. *The Urban Daily.* https://theurbandaily.com/587122/eulogy-thoughts-on-the-death-of-biggie-smalls

Gershenson, S. & Papageorge, N. (2018). The power of teacher expectations. *Education Next, (18)*1. https://www.educationnext.org/power-of-teacher-expectations-racial-bias-hinders-student-attainment

Hussar, B., NCES; Zhang, J., Hein, S., Wang, K., Roberts, A., Cui, J., Smith, M., AIR; Bullock Mann, F., Barmer, A., & Dilig, R., RTI. (2020, May). *The Condition of Education 2020.* National Center for Education Statistics. https://nces.ed.gov/pubsearch/pubsinfo.asp?pubid=2020144

Johnson, M. P. (2008). *A typology of domestic violence: Intimate, terrorism, violent resistance, and situational couple violence.* Northeastern University Press.

McLeod, S. A. (2018). Erik Erikson's stages of psychosocial development. *Simply Psychology.* https://www.simplypsychology.org/Erik-Erikson.html

Wallace, C. (1994). Juicy [Song]. On *Ready to Die.* The Hit Factory.

"Instructional Equity: What, Why, and How" (page 75)

Judd, D. & Nobles, R. (2020, October 17). Georgia Republican senator willfully mispronounces Kamala Harris' name at Trump rally. *CNN.* https://www.cnn.com/2020/10/16/politics/david-perdue-kamala-harris/index.html

Learning for Justice. (n.d.) *Social justice standards: A framework for anti-bias education.* https://www.learningforjustice.org/frameworks/social-justice-standards

Minor, Cornelius. (2018). *We got this. Equity, access, and the quest to be who our students need us to be.* Heinemann.

National Center for Education Statistics. (2021). ACS-ED *District demographic dashboard 2015–19.* Education Demographics and Geographic Estimates. https://nces.ed.gov/Programs/Edge/ACSDashboard/4102040

Native Land Digital. (2022). https://native-land.ca

Oregon's Kid Governor. (2022). http://or.kidgovernor.org

Security.org Team (2019, October 4). *32 cities.* https://www.security.org/resources/homeless-statistics-2019

Wich, K. (2014, October 18). *Moving from kindness to justice: Creating social change in the elementary classroom* [Workshop session]. Northwest Teaching for Social Justice Conference, Portland, OR.

Willingham, A. J. (2019, October 14). These states and cities are ditching Columbus Day to observe Indigenous Peoples' Day instead. *CNN.* https://www.cnn.com/2019/04/22/us/indigenous-peoples-day-columbus-day-trnd/index.html

"Spotlight on Third-Grade Literacy Proficiency for Black and Brown Youth" (page 88)

Brown, M. C., Sibley, D. E., Washington, J. A., Rogers, T. T., Edwards, J. R., MacDonald, M. C., & Seidenberg, M. S. (2015, March 24). Impact of dialect use on a basic component of learning to read. *Frontiers in Psychology, (6)*196. https://doi.org/10.3389/fpsyg.2015.00196

Gough, P. & Tunmer, W. (1986). Decoding, reading, and reading disability. *Remedial and special education, (7),* 6–10. https://doi.org/10.1177/074193258600700104

Hanford, E. (2020, August 6). *What the words say.* APM Reports. https://www.apmreports.org/episode/2020/08/06/what-the-words-say

Kids Count Data Center. (2022). *Fourth grade reading achievement levels in the United States.* https://datacenter.kidscount.org/data/tables/5116-fourth-grade-reading-achievement-levels

Kids Count Data Center. (2022). *Fourth graders who scored below proficient reading level by race in the United States.* https://datacenter.kidscount.org/data/tables/5126-fourth-graders-who-scored-below-proficient-reading-level-by-race

Morgan, P. L., Farkas, G., & Wu, Q. (2012). Do poor readers feel angry, sad, and unpopular? *Scientific Studies of Reading, 16*(4), 360–381. https://doi.org/10.1080/10888438.2011.570397

Ordetx, K. (2021). What is the science of reading? *IMSE Journal*. https://journal.imse.com/what-is-the-science-of-reading

Torgesen, J. K. (2004). *Avoiding the devastating downward spiral*. American Federation of Teachers. https://www.aft.org/periodical/american-educator/fall-2004/avoiding-devastating-downward-spiral

Stoltzfus, K. (2021). *'Last year was a wake-up call': Family engagement after COVID-19*. ASCD. https://www.ascd.org/blogs/last-year-was-a-wake-up-call-family-engagement-after-covid-19

"Equity and Justice in the Classroom and Beyond" (page 96)

Brown, A. M. & Imaresha, W. (Eds.) (2015). *Octavia's brood: Science fiction stories from social justice movements*. AK Press.

Dewar, G. (2012). Teaching critical thinking: An evidence-based guide. *Parenting Science*. https://parentingscience.com/teaching-critical-thinking

Duncan, A. (2018). Education: The "Great Equalizer." *Encyclopedia Britannica*. https://www.britannica.com/topic/Education-The-Great-Equalizer-2119678

EdBuild. (2019, February). *$23 billion*. https://edbuild.org/content/23-billion

Gorman, A. (2021). *The hill we climb: An inaugural poem for the country*. Viking Books.

Pettit, S. K., Albert, C. D., Walker, J., & Rychly, L. (2017). Young citizens of the world unite! A case for the model United Nations in middle school classrooms. *Middle Grades Review, 3*(2). https://scholarworks.uvm.edu/mgreview/vol3/iss2/2

Ross, D. (2020, February 11). Strategies for cultivating a classroom that represents students. *Responsive Classroom*. https://www.responsiveclassroom.org/strategies-for-cultivating-a-classroom-that-represents-students

Stevenson, B. (2015). *Just mercy: A story of justice and redemption*. One World.

Weissberg, R., Durlak, J. A., Domitrovich, C. E., & Gullotta, T. P. (2016, February 15). Why social and emotional learning is essential for students. *Edutopia*. https://www.edutopia.org/blog/why-sel-essential-for-students-weissberg-durlak-domitrovich-gullotta

"Young pupils allegedly forced to re-enact Holocaust in Washington school." (2021, December 20). *BBC News*. https://www.bbc.com/news/world-us-canada-59733807

Zinn, H. & Steforff, R. (2009). *A young people's history of the United States: Columbus to the war on terror*. Triangle Square.

"Maximizing Field Trips to Close Opportunity Gaps" (page 113)

Alper, S. (2020). Educational equity and informal STEM field trip programming. *Master's Theses*. 1288.

Behrendt, M., & Franklin T. (2014). A review of research on school field trips and their value in education. *International Journal of Environmental and Science Education, 9*(3), 235–245. https://eric.ed.gov/?id=EJ1031445

DeWitt, J., Storksdieck, M. (2008). A short review of school field trips: Key findings from the past and implications for the future. *Visitor Studies. 11*(2), 181–197. https://doi.org/10.1080/10645570802355562

National Education Association. (n.d.) How field trips boost students' lifelong success. *NEA Member Benefits*. https://www.neamb.com/work-life/how-field-trips-boost-students-lifelong-success

Peetz, C. (2019, February 4). Inequities discovered in student field trips. *Bethesda Beat*. https://bethesdamagazine.com/bethesda-beat/inequities-discovered-in-student-field-trips

Poiner, J. (2015, November 3). *The opportunity gap: Extracurricular and field trips aren't just for fun*. Thomas B. Fordham Institute. https://fordhaminstitute.org/ohio/commentary/opportunity-gap-extracurriculars-and-field-trips-arent-just-fun

Putnam, R. D. (2016). *Our kids: The American dream in crisis*. Simon & Schuster.

Whitesell, E. R. (2016). A day at the museum: The impact of field trips on middle school science achievement. *Journal of Research in Science Teaching, (53)*7, 1036–1054. https://doi.org/10.1002/tea.21322